T0012642

WHAT FOLKS SAID ABOUT *STILL RISING* AND EARLIER EDITIONS OF *FAMOUS BLACK QUOTATIONS*

"*STILL RISING* OFFERS creative, personable guidance and wisdom to all people, from the youngest of aspiring Black women to those of us stepping into our power as civic leaders."

JUDITH THOMAS
deputy mayor of neighborhood engagement,
City of Indianapolis

"THERE IS NOTHING like a timely, well-placed quote to make one's writing, speaking, or presentations sparkle. And to find that perfect quote, there is no more convenient or easy-to-use source than *Famous Black Quotations*. . . . Highly recommended."

THE BLACK COLLEGIAN

"JANET CHEATHAM BELL has extracted the best from the best and packed it all into one small but powerful space!"

LES BROWN
motivational speaker

"EVERYWHERE I GO all over this country, African American leaders are using *Famous Black Quotations*."

JEREMIAH A. WRIGHT JR.
pastor emeritus, Trinity United Church of Christ, Chicago

"*Famous Black Quotations* is a valuable resource."

"It is an excellent and much-needed addition to the literature."

"An invaluable reference. . . . The book provides a saying of substance for a variety of occasions. *Famous Black Quotations* is truly a godsend."

"*Famous Black Quotations* is right here in my study; I use it all the time."

"Janet Cheatham Bell is a pioneer in doing books of Black quotations."

STILL RISING

STILL RISING

FAMOUS BLACK QUOTATIONS
FOR THE
TWENTY-FIRST
CENTURY

JANET CHEATHAM BELL

A BOLDEN BOOK

AGATE

CHICAGO

First printed in 2023

Printed in the United States of America

10 9 8 7 6 5 4 3 2 1   23 24 25 26 27

Author photo by Merridee LaMantia

Library of Congress Cataloging-in-Publication Data
Names: Bell, Janet Cheatham, editor.
Title: Still rising: famous Black quotations for the twenty-first century
 / [selected and compiled by] Janet Cheatham Bell.
Description: Chicago : Bolden Books, [2023]
Identifiers: LCCN 2022019163 (print) | LCCN 2022019164 (ebook) | ISBN
 9781572843202 (hardcover) | ISBN 9781572848719 (ebook)
Subjects: LCSH: African Americans--Quotations. | Blacks--Quotations.
Classification: LCC PN6081.3 .F364 2023 (print) | LCC PN6081.3 (eb-
ook)|
 DDC 081/.08996073--dc23/eng/20220520
LC record available at https://lccn.loc.gov/2022019163
LC ebook record available at https://lccn.loc.gov/2022019164

Bolden is an imprint of Agate Publishing. Agate books are available in bulk at discount prices. For more information, visit agatepublishing.com.

COMPARISONS OF HUMAN genes worldwide have produced a "family tree" of the human race whose branches closely mirror the branching of languages proposed by linguists, leading to the startling suggestion that all people—and perhaps all languages—are descended from a tiny population that lived in Africa some 200,000 years ago.

WILLIAM F. ALLMAN
U.S. News & World Report
November 5, 1990

[THE RESPONSE TO the January 6 insurrection] is a story about what we agree to remember and what we choose to forget, about how history is not lived but manufactured after the fact.

MOLLY BALL
"What Mike Fanone Can't Forget," *Time*
August 5, 2021

BLACK PEOPLE WILL always ensure this nation lives up to its ideals of liberty and justice, freedom and equity for all. We are on the precipice of true structural change—a change for which thousands of Black lives have fought, marched and died. But freedom is a constant struggle and we can't stop fighting. We must keep moving forward. There is no other way.

EPILOGUE TO THE NAACP'S *TWENTY20 IN BLACK*

CONTENTS

FOREWORD
BY W. KAMAU BELL

You know those quotes that you Google on the internet? Somebody at some point found those quotes. And you know that quote, "Where there's life, there's hope," that you thought was by Socrates or Plato, but actually was by Terence (Publius Terentius Afer) from North Africa? There is somebody out there who could have told you that before you went around sharing it with everybody. Well, my mom is one of those people, especially when it relates to quotes by Black folks. And she doesn't care whose feelings she hurts in the process. One time she came to my kids' school, and on the back wall of the gymnasium there were large drawings done by a student of legendary Black people. One of them was President Barack Obama. And below his drawing was a quote. My mom looked at it, turned to me, and said, "He's not the one who said that." I looked back at her like she was going to ruin the whole assembly if word got out. I imagined my mom standing up during the assembly and loudly telling everyone to stop what they were doing because she saw a grievous error. I imagined the school calling the kid to the front of the assembly at that moment and then ordering the student to destroy the drawing in front of all of us.

None of that happened. But it was a reminder to me that the work my mom does isn't a thing she decided to do. It is a calling. She feels compelled beyond logic and common sense to connect us all—and Black people specifically—to our higher selves. To our better selves. To our smarter selves. To our more evolved, more revolutionary selves. To be more in line with the ancestors who fought and died for the freedom of Black people in the United States of America. And my mom knew that she didn't have to invent a way for this to happen. She could just circulate the wisdom that Black folks had already put out into the universe. And for my mom, these weren't just inspirational words. These were little history lessons. My mom doesn't just want you to know what Oprah Winfrey said. She wants you to know *what* she said, *where* and *why* she said it, and *who* she said it to.

When my mom began to self-publish her *Famous Black Quotations* books in the mid-'80s, there were certainly books that collected quotes, but they were not entire books of quotations by people of African descent. And I saw my mom create an industry out of our apartment in Chicago. She traveled all around the Chicagoland area finding graphic designers, printers, and typesetters to make her dream of a pocket-sized book of bite-sized African American wisdom come true. And then she called all around the country to the network of Black bookstores that understood that some of their most popular books would not come from the major publishers. They would come from Black people directly. These were Black people like my mom who weren't gonna wait for some New York publisher to say that they were good enough. They did what Black folks always and still do. They did it themselves. My mom paid our rent, put food on the table, and put me through school by selling these books. And even though she is eighty-five years old, and now I'm the one working for her, she feels the call to once again share the wisdom. And we are all the better for it. Because even though we can all Google our way to "inspirational Black quotes," it is always way better if someone has done the work of making sure where that quote is coming from and giving you the context around it. And nobody is better at that than my mom. We are all lucky that at eighty-five she still feels that calling.

Anyway, I have to call my kids' school about that quote.

A NOTE
FROM THE CURATOR

I self-published my first collection of quotations by people of African descent in 1986. It was so popular that in 1992 I published a second collection. With the help of my son, W. Kamau Bell (then a teen), we sold over ninety thousand copies of those two pocket-sized books. I licensed both to Warner Books (now Grand Central Publishing), who combined them and published *Famous Black Quotations* in 1995. Brisk sales continued. Then the world wide web happened, changing everything. It seemed people were primarily obtaining information from the internet. By 2008 *Famous Black Quotations* was out of print.

I discovered, to my annoyance, that much of what was on the internet was incorrect. Some quotations were worded inaccurately or attributed to the wrong person, but I had moved on to write essays and memoirs. (My other publications are listed at the end of this book.) A friend insisted there is still a need for *Famous Black Quotations* and suggested that I publish it again and promote it on social media. I examined the 1995 edition and decided it couldn't be republished without an update. I needed to add the words of people not included in earlier editions—like the Obamas, Nikole Hannah-Jones, and Colin Kaepernick.

In earlier editions of *Famous Black Quotations*, I did not include dates, sources, or biographical information for the people quoted. In this iteration, however, appropriate dates and brief identifiers are included. These identifiers can serve as a guide to the evolution of our history and experiences. They can also lead to further study of these eloquent history makers and thought leaders from throughout the African Diaspora. I've made editorial decisions, where appropriate, to convert male pronouns that refer to people as a whole to gender-neutral terms. I also capitalize Black because it refers to a specific cultural group.

Obviously, this collection is not exhaustive or comprehensive, yet I have attempted to include a range of thought, limited, of course, by my human inability to read everything and be everywhere. It does, however, include people of African descent from throughout the Diaspora, past and present. Most of these quotations are culled from primary sources, both printed and oral. However, there are some from secondary sources that perhaps introduce errors. As well, I may have copied something incorrectly. Efforts have been made to obtain permission for quotations not in public domain or fair use. If you are misquoted in this book, or can document other factual errors, please send corrections and additional data to me at **janetcheathambell.com**.

QUOTATIONS ARE USEFUL in a variety of ways. They can be read for education and inspiration. They can add weight and heft to otherwise uninspired writing. And they can powerfully and poignantly say for the speaker or writer what [they] might not be able to summon without assistance.

JULIAN BOND in the foreword to
*Till Victory Is Won: Famous Black Quotations from the
NAACP* (2002)

ABBREVIATIONS

ACLU = American Civil Liberties Union

AFI = American Film Institute

BET = Black Entertainment Television

CNN = Cable News Network

EGOT = Emmy, Grammy, Oscar, Tony

ESPN = Entertainment and Sports Programming Network

ESPY = Excellence in Sports Performance Yearly

NAACP = National Association for the Advancement of Colored People

NASA = National Aeronautics and Space Administration

NBA = National Basketball Association

NPR = National Public Radio

NFL = National Football League

OWN = Oprah Winfrey Network

PBS = Public Broadcasting Service

SCLC = Southern Christian Leadership Council

SNCC = Student Nonviolent Coordinating Committee (pronounced "Snick")

UPS = United Parcel Service

U.S. = United States

WNBA = Women's National Basketball Association

WTA = Women's Tennis Association

STRUGGLE
RESISTING WHITE SUPREMACY

If there is no struggle, there is no progress.

FREDERICK DOUGLASS

IN A BID for change, we have to take off our coats, be prepared to lose our comfort and security, our jobs and positions of prestige, and our families. . . . A struggle without casualties is no struggle.

STEPHEN BIKO (1946–1977)
founder, South Africa's Black Consciousness
Movement (1969)

NOTIONS OF WHITE superiority that were created in the 15th century to justify conquest and slavery have a firm grip on the minds of people of all colors.

MARK P. FANCHER in "Where Incarceration Isn't
the Answer," *YES! The Better Ideas Issue*, Fall 2020;
human rights attorney, writer

THERE WAS ONE of two things I had a right to, liberty or death; if I could not have one, I would have the other. I would fight for my liberty so long as my strength lasted, and if the time came for me to go, the Lord would let them take me.

HARRIET TUBMAN (c.1820–1913)
born into slavery, escaped, and led others to freedom
via the Underground Railroad

I WOULD NEVER be of any service to anyone as a slave.

> NAT TURNER (1800–1831) in *The Confessions of Nat Turner* (1831); executed for leading a rebellion against slavers

IF THERE IS no struggle, there is no progress. . . . This struggle may be a moral one or a physical one . . . or it may be both, but it must be a struggle. Power concedes nothing without a demand. It never has and it never will.

> FREDERICK DOUGLASS (1817–1895) in *Narrative of the Life of Frederick Douglass, an American Slave* (1845); enslaved until age nineteen, abolitionist, orator, author

THE PROBLEM OF the twentieth century is the problem of the color line.

> W. E. B. DU BOIS (1868–1963) in *The Souls of Black Folk* (1903); author; professor; co-founder, NAACP

WHITE SUPREMACY DON'T got a passport. White supremacy doesn't stop at the border. White supremacy is a global system. . . . I fight for the rights of people who are vulnerable, no matter where they are.

> MARC LAMONT HILL on *The Breakfast Club*, March 2021; professor, Temple University; co-author of *Except for Palestine: The Limits of Progressive Politics* (2021)

WHITE SUPREMACY EXISTS within the Left too. . . . [Radical white abolitionist William Lloyd] Garrison and [Frederick] Douglass ended their partnership over this and other issues. But the idea that white progressives can tell Black activists what to do is still a problem in the protest movement.

JAMON JORDAN in "Rebellions Work," *YES! The Black Lives Issue*, Fall 2020; educator, writer, historian

MANY LIBERALS WHO say that "Defund the police" goes too far don't want to admit that while they say Black Lives Matter, they still want a mechanism to keep Black people in check.

IJEOMA OLUO in a December 2020 tweet; author of *So You Want to Talk About Race* (2018)

A LOT OF Black cops are blue first and Black second, and that mentality has them viewing Black children through the same lens of whiteness America has always viewed Black youth through.

ZACK LINLY in "Mother Sues Maryland County. . .," *The Root*, March 2021; poet, performer, freelance writer, community organizer

PEOPLE ARE IGNORANT of the things that affect their actions, yet they rarely *feel* ignorant.

MALCOLM GLADWELL in *Blink: The Power of Thinking Without Thinking* (2005); author of *The Tipping Point* (2000), journalist

THE MILLION MAN March/Day of Abstinence [in 1995] was a classic example of operational unity. It also was important because it came at a time when there was a massive silence in America about rising white supremacy and a tendency to return to the old raw, racist days of blaming the victims.

MAULANA KARENGA in a PBS interview, 1997; creator of Kwanzaa, Africana studies scholar, author

WHAT [DOES] IT mean to live in a country where fear was being weaponized against certain people in our society, and where I myself was both at risk of performing this mode of racial profiling, even as I am a target of this same form of projected and weaponized fear?

CLAUDIA RANKINE in the *Los Angeles Review of Books*; 2016 MacArthur Fellow, award-winning poet, essayist, playwright, author of *Citizen* (2014) and *Just Us* (2020)

I AM NOT going to stand up to show pride in a flag for a country that oppresses Black people and people of color. To me, this is bigger than football and it would be selfish on my part to look the other way. There are bodies in the street and people getting paid leave and getting away with murder.

COLIN KAEPERNICK after he refused to stand for the
national anthem, 2016;
quarterback, San Francisco 49ers (2011–16); *Sports Illustrated* Muhammad Ali Legacy Award winner (2017)

AS A BLACK woman I feel as though there are much more important things at hand that need immediate attention, rather than watching me play tennis. I don't expect anything drastic to happen with me not playing, but if I can get a conversation started in a majority white sport, I consider that a step in the right direction.

NAOMI OSAKA in an August 2020 tweet;
a top-ranked world WTA player; ESPY Best Female
Athlete Award winner (2021); social justice advocate

LET YOUR MOTTO be resistance! resistance! RESISTANCE! No oppressed people have ever secured their liberty without resistance.

HENRY HIGHLAND GARNET (1815–1882)
enslaved until age nine, abolitionist, educator, minister

YOU CAN JAIL a Revolutionary, but you can't jail the Revolution.

FRED HAMPTON (1948–1969)
co-founder and chair, Illinois Black Panther Party;
revolutionary strategist and organizer

I HAVE CHERISHED the ideal of a democratic and free society in which all persons live together in harmony with equal opportunities. It is an ideal which I hope to live for and to see realized. But, if needs be, it is an ideal for which I am prepared to die.

ROLIHLAHLA NELSON MANDELA (1918–2013)
incarcerated for resisting apartheid (1963–90),
president of South Africa (1994–99)

[BLACK PEOPLE ARE] supposed to sit passively, and have no feelings, be non-violent, and love [the] enemy, no matter what kind of attack, be it verbal or otherwise, [we're] supposed to take it. But if [we] stand up and, in any way, try to defend [ourselves], then [we're] extremists.

MALCOLM X/el-Hajj Malik el-Shabazz (1925–1965) at
an Oxford University Student Union debate, 1964;
National Representative of the Nation of Islam;
founder, Organization of Afro-American Unity

You can kill me, but you can never kill what I stand for. You can never erase that demonstration.

JOHN CARLOS on *Soul of a Nation*, March 2021; Black Power salute with Tommie Smith on Olympic medal stand (1968), co-author of *The John Carlos Story* (1994)

The first time I got arrested demonstrating . . . for speaking up and speaking out against segregation and racial discrimination, I felt free. I felt liberated. . . . It made me a stronger and better person. And eventually, because of the civil rights movement, America became stronger and better.

JOHN LEWIS (1940–2020) in the afterword of *His Truth Is Marching On* by Jon Meacham (2020); U.S. representative (1987–2020); chair, SNCC (1963–66)

Because of [the civil rights] movement, people have a seat at the table. . . . Because of that movement, America has changed for the better.

DONNA BRAZILE on *Black America Since MLK: And Still I Rise* (2016); political strategist, campaign manager, political analyst

I BECAME INTERESTED in the civil rights struggle out of the necessity to survive.

SIDNEY POITIER (1927–2022)
author, director, award-winning actor

THE EASY ANSWER is that the civil rights movement was to secure the rights of American citizens for Black Americans, but it was much, much more. The struggle the Black community and its allies waged . . . deepened the currents of American democracy for all Americans.

EKWUEME MICHAEL THELWELL on The Choices
Program, Brown University, 2012;
author; professor; founding chair, Department of
Afro-American Studies, University of Massachusetts

THE PAST FOUR years have indeed been a crime scene in which the America of the U.S. Constitution has been duct-taped to a chair and relentlessly waterboarded by those chanting "Make America Great Again."

KAREEM ABDUL-JABBAR in the *Hollywood Reporter*,
October 2020;
author of *Becoming Kareem* (2017), recipient of Presidential Medal of Freedom (2016), Basketball Hall of
Fame inductee (1995)

THERE IS THE sense in which there is a flooding of consciousness in the society. And what happens whenever you have an oppressive leader and oppressive accessories to the crime of oppression . . . who just continue to press people down—eventually that pressing-down overflows. It spews out. People can't take it anymore, and won't take it.

> WILLIAM J. BARBER II in *The Atlantic*, November 2020;
> leader of Moral Mondays; author; pastor, Greenleaf
> Christian Church; president, North Carolina NAACP

WE BEEN SAYING "freedom" for six years. What we are going to start saying now is "Black Power."

> STOKELY CARMICHAEL/KWAME TURE (1941–1998)
> at the Mississippi "Walk Against Fear," 1966;
> chair, SNCC (1966–67); founder, Lowndes County
> Black Panther Party

THE MOVEMENTS WE'RE witnessing now are direct descendants of the movements of the past.

> YARA SHAHIDI in *Vanity Fair*, September 2020;
> actor (*Blackish*, *Grownish*), social justice advocate

THEORY DOES NOT solve issues—only action and solidarity can do that—but theory gives you language to fight, knowledge to stand on, and a humbling reality of what intersectional social justice is up against.

> BETTINA LOVE in *We Want to Do More Than Survive* (2019); professor, University of Georgia; founder, Abolitionist Teaching Network; creator, GET FREE Hip Hop civics curriculum

HASHTAGS DO NOT start movements—people do. Movements do not have official moments when they start and end, and there is never just one person who initiates them. . . . We inherit movements. We recommit to them over and over again even when they break our hearts, because they are essential to our survival.

> ALICIA GARZA in *The Purpose of Power* (2020); co-founder, Black Lives Matter (2013); organizer; political strategist

THE REASON THERE'S unrest in our streets is because there's unrest in the lives of Black Americans, and that's across every issue.

> AYANNA PRESSLEY in *Vanity Fair*, September 2020; U.S. representative (2019–)

[THE CIVIL RIGHTS movement] had a positive economic impact . . . for middle-class Blacks. The civil rights victories really did not have much of a positive impact on the Black poor.

WILLIAM JULIUS WILSON on *Black America Since MLK: And Still I Rise* (2016); sociologist; professor, Harvard University; author of *When Work Disappears* (1996)

OUR STRENGTH IS that with the total society saying to us, *"No, No, No,"* we continue to move toward our goal. So when I came to write I felt moved to affirm and to explore all this.

RALPH ELLISON (1913–1994) in *Shadow and Act* (1964); author of *Invisible Man* (1952) and *Going to the Territory* (1986), National Book Award winner (1953)

THIS IS A marathon for justice. . . . You have to keep fighting, you have to run this lap of the race. Ron Dellums passed me the baton, we passed younger people the batons. We see Black Lives Matter and Dreamers. We see . . . everyone coming together now, taking these batons and running with it!

BARBARA LEE in an interview with *The Nation*, August 2020; author of *Renegade for Peace and Justice* (2008), lone member of Congress to vote against the 2001 U.S. invasion of Afghanistan, U.S. representative (1998–)

I DON'T KNOW of anything in the history of Black people in this country in which I've read some account which ended with, "and then they gave up." That's just not what we do. . . . We work for the future of our children and our grandchildren and their children.

SHERRILYN IFILL in a June 2020 tweet;
author of *On the Courthouse Lawn* (2007); president
and director-counsel, NAACP Legal Defense and
Educational Fund (2013–22)

WE MUST NEVER surrender. America will get better and better. Keep hope alive.

JESSE JACKSON at the 1988 Democratic
National Convention;
candidate for U.S. president (1984, 1988); founder,
Rainbow/PUSH Coalition; author of *Keeping Hope
Alive* (2019) and *Legal Lynching* (1996)

FIGHT THE POWER. We've got to fight the powers that be.

PUBLIC ENEMY, rap group, 1989

A COMMUNITY IS democratic only when the humblest and weakest person can enjoy the highest civil, economic, and social rights that the biggest and most powerful possess.

A. PHILIP RANDOLPH (1889–1979)
founder, Brotherhood of Sleeping Car Porters labor
union (1925)

THE MOST DIFFICULT and urgent challenge today is that of creatively exploring new terrains of justice, where the prison no longer serves as our major anchor.

ANGELA Y. DAVIS in *Are Prisons Obsolete?* (2003);
professor emerita, University of California, Santa
Cruz; author of *Freedom Is a Constant Struggle* (2015);
social justice advocate

SEXISM HAS DIMINISHED the power of all Black liberation struggles—reformist or revolutionary.

BELL HOOKS/Gloria Watkins (1952–2021) in *Yearning: Race, Gender, and Cultural Politics* (1990);
author; professor; feminist theorist; founder,
bell hooks Institute

THE MASTER'S TOOLS will never dismantle the master's house.

AUDRE LORDE (1934–1992)
Black, lesbian, mother, warrior, poet, author of
Sister Outsider (1984)

IT . . . OCCURRED TO me that a system of oppression draws much of its strength from the acquiescence of its victims who have accepted the dominant image of themselves and are paralyzed by a sense of helplessness.

> **PAULI MURRAY** (1910–1985) in *Song in a Weary Throat* (1987);
> author of *Proud Shoes* (1956); social justice advocate;
> co-founder, National Organization for Women; poet;
> lawyer; Episcopal priest

IT HAS NOT been easy being a citizen in this country . . . [which] unleashed a war on its own citizens just because we wanted to be free.

> **PATRICIA STEPHENS DUE** (1939–2012) on C-SPAN's *Book TV*, January 2003;
> co-author of *Freedom in the Family* (2003), pioneer
> Florida social justice advocate

I THANK GOD! I thank God on this day that I do not have a son! Because if I had a son I would have sent him out to war on this day.

> **DRUSILLA DUNJEE HOUSTON** (1876–1941) as bombs
> were being dropped on Tulsa, OK;
> journalist, author of *Wonderful Ethiopians of the Ancient Cushite Empire* (1926)

ANY ATTEMPT THE Black [person] makes to be seen or heard, clearly, honestly, from where [they have] been made to live during the three-hundred-odd year residency in the West, is always met with repression and violence.

AMIRI BARAKA/LEROI JONES (1934–2014) in *Home: Social Essays* (1966); playwright, poet, essayist

I FELT THAT one had better die fighting against injustice than to die like a dog or a rat in a trap. I had already determined to sell my life as dearly as possible if attacked.

IDA B. WELLS-BARNETT (1862–1931) in *Crusade for Justice: The Autobiography of Ida B. Wells*, edited by Alfreda Duster (1970); journalist; anti-lynching advocate; co-founder, NAACP

I'M SICK AND tired of being sick and tired.

FANNIE LOU HAMER (1917–1977) an organizer of the "Freedom Summer" voter registration drive (1964); co-founder, Mississippi Freedom Democratic Party

IF ROSA PARKS had taken a poll before she sat down in the bus in Montgomery, she'd still be standing.

MARY FRANCES BERRY chair, U.S. Commission on Civil Rights (1993–2004); professor; author of *History Teaches Us to Resist* (2018)

THROUGH THE CENTURIES of despair and dislocation, we had been creative, because we faced down death by daring to hope.

> MAYA ANGELOU (1928–2014) in *Wouldn't Take Nothing for My Journey Now* (1993); poet, performer, author, social justice advocate

[THAT NEWS COMMENTATOR] helped me create more awareness. . . . I will not "shut up and dribble." I mean too much to my family and all those other kids who look up to me for inspiration and to find a way out.

> LEBRON JAMES at the 2018 NBA All-Star Weekend; member of the L.A. Lakers, four-time NBA champion, social justice advocate

THERE WAS NEVER a honeymoon period for affirmative action. . . . There's never been a period where any effort to integrate African Americans into American society was not immediately denounced as preferential treatment.

> KIMBERLÉ CRENSHAW on *Black America Since MLK: And Still I Rise* (2016); professor of law at UCLA and Columbia Law School

WE'VE BEEN FLOATING this country on credit for centuries, and we're done watching and waiting while this invention called whiteness uses and abuses us, burying Black people out of sight and out of mind while extracting our culture, our dollars, our entertainment like oil—black gold, ghettoizing and demeaning our creations then stealing them, gentrifying our genius and then trying us on like costumes before discarding our bodies like rinds of strange fruit.

> **JESSE WILLIAMS** accepting the BET Humanitarian
> Award, 2016;
> actor, producer

SHARECROPPING WAS STRICTLY another form of slavery. . . . Hope is the only thing that keeps [Black farmers] going.

> **WILL SCOTT JR.** on *Our America: Living While Black*, 2021;
> fourth-generation farmer, Scott Family Farms in
> Fresno, California

WE WORKED UNTIL the job was done or until we couldn't work anymore. And even when we'd done everything we could, that didn't mean . . . a damn thing.

> **WALTER MOSLEY** in *Black Betty* (1994);
> author of *A Red Death* (1991), *Devil in a Blue Dress*
> (1990), and other Easy Rawlins mysteries

FOR BLACK PEOPLE, dirt will never be just one thing. There will always be a tension between soil and tradition, soil and progress, soil and freedom. We garden to reconcile that tension. . . . Gardening is our attempt to remember and forget, look ahead and reach back, hold tight and push forward.

> NATALIE BASZILE in *National Geographic*, 2021;
> author of *We Are Each Other's Harvest* (2021) and
> *Queen Sugar* (2014); food justice advocate

THE WHOLE IDEA that soul food is just slave food breaks down pretty easily once you start applying some historical scrutiny to it.

> ADRIAN MILLER in *Stanford* magazine, March 2021;
> executive director, Colorado Council of Churches;
> culinary historian; barbecue judge; lawyer; public policy advisor; author of *Black Smoke* (2021), *The President's Kitchen Cabinet* (2017), and *Soul Food* (2013)

WE HAVE SURVIVED and continue to survive because as artists and activists, as storytellers and change-makers of all kinds, we know that no matter how crazy and deadly a moment seems, we continue to stare the future down in order to show the way to it.

> JACQUELINE WOODSON in *Vanity Fair*, November 2020;
> children's book author, 2020 MacArthur Fellow

I HOPE TO be a voice for the African American community in the pope's ear.

WILTON GREGORY in the *Washington Post*,
November 28, 2020;
cardinal, Roman Catholic Church

IF WE THROW all those [Republican voters] away, it turns out there is no AWAY! We're all still HERE! Who suffers if we keep the food fight going? . . . We've got to remember that the people who suffer the most are the people at the bottom—the addicted, the convicted, the afflicted, the young.

VAN JONES on *The View*, February 5, 2021;
news commentator, lawyer, author of *Beyond the
Messy Truth* (2017)

WHEN ELEPHANTS FIGHT it is the grass that suffers.

KIKUYU PROVERB

STRATEGY IS BETTER than strength.

HAUSA PROVERB

AND STILL YOU are called to struggle, not because it assures you victory but because it assures you an honorable and sane life.

> **TA-NEHISI COATES** in *Between the World and Me* (2015);
> author, essayist, journalist, 2015 MacArthur Fellow

TAKE PRIDE IN knowing that your struggle will play the biggest role in your purpose.

> **MARCUS RASHFORD** at the 2021 ESPY Awards;
> recipient of Pat Tillman Award for Service (2021);
> member, Manchester United and the England
> national football team

YOU HAVE TO understand that people have to pay a price for peace. If you dare to struggle, you dare to win.

> **FRED HAMPTON** (1948–1969)
> co-founder and chair, Illinois Black Panther Party;
> revolutionary strategist and organizer

IDENTITY
DEFINING OURSELVES

If I didn't define myself for myself, I would be
crunched into other people's fantasies . . .

AUDRE LORDE

ONE EVER FEELS his two-ness—an American, a Negro; two souls, two thoughts, two unreconciled strivings; two warring ideals in one dark body, whose dogged strength alone keeps it from being torn asunder.

W. E. B. DU BOIS (1868–1963) in *The Souls of Black Folk* (1903); co-founder, NAACP; author; professor

I DON'T HAVE a "double consciousness." I am who I am. I'm the first comic to bring a "just between us" Black voice to the stage, to any stage, any audience, white, Black, or mixed.

PAUL MOONEY (1941–2021) in *Black Is the New White* (2009); comedian, writer, actor

MOULDED ON AFRICA'S anvil, tempered down home.

JULIAN BOND (1940–2015) in "The Bishop of Atlanta: Ray Charles"; co-founder, SNCC; co-founder, Southern Poverty Law Center; essayist; poet; national chair, NAACP (1998–2009)

AFRICA'S AGRICULTURAL KNOW-HOW rendered the fields of the New World more productive, while Africa's recipes morphed, took on New World inflections, and transformed the tastes of a hemisphere.

JESSICA B. HARRIS in "Out of Africa," *Black Food* (2021); culinary historian, professor, journalist, author of *My Soul Looks Back* (2017), *High on the Hog* (2011), and *The Welcome Table* (1995)

WHAT COULD I dream of that had the barest possibility of coming true? I could think of nothing. And, slowly, it was upon exactly that nothingness that my mind began to dwell, that constant sense of wanting without having, of being hated without reason.

RICHARD WRIGHT (1908–1960) in *American Hunger* (1944); author of *White Man, Listen!* (1957), *Black Boy* (1945), and *Native Son* (1940); social justice advocate

TREASURE YOUR CURIOSITY, nurture your imagination. Have confidence in yourself. Do not let others put limits on you. Dare to imagine the unimaginable.

SHIRLEY ANN JACKSON theoretical physicist; president, Rensselaer Polytechnic Institute; member, President's Council of Advisors on Science and Technology (2009–14); chair, U.S. Nuclear Regulatory Commission (1995–99)

I HAD TO stand up in different ways throughout my life. I mean, being a Black woman . . . most Black women have moments in life where they just have to stand and take on whatever is coming at you because you know it's wrong.

BARBARA LEE in *Esquire*, August 2021;
author of *Renegade for Peace and Justice* (2008), lone
member of Congress to vote against the 2001 U.S.
invasion of Afghanistan, U.S. representative (1998–)

I'VE LIVED TO see my lost causes [equal rights for Blacks and women] found.

PAULI MURRAY (1910–1985) on *My Name Is Pauli
Murray* (2021);
author of *Song in a Weary Throat* (1987) and *Proud Shoes*
(1956); social justice advocate; co-founder, National
Organization for Women; poet; lawyer; Episcopal priest

ORDINARY PEOPLE CAN do extraordinary things.

PATRICIA STEPHENS DUE (1939–2012)
co-author of *Freedom in the Family* (2003), pioneer
Florida social justice advocate

EACH OF US are unique expressions of the infinite . . . always on a journey of unfolding.

MICHAEL BERNARD BECKWITH on *Super Soul Sunday*;
founder, Agape International Spiritual Center; author
of *True Abundance* (2010)

THE SINGLE STORY creates stereotypes, and the problem with stereotypes is not that they are untrue, but that they are incomplete. They make one story become the only story.

> **CHIMAMANDA NGOZI ADICHIE** in TED Talk, "The Danger of a Single Story," July 2009; award-winning author, 2008 MacArthur Fellow

WHAT WOULD YOU do if you knew you were worthy?

> **INDIA.ARIE** Simpson musical artist, songwriter, Grammy Award winner, NAACP Image Award winner

START ENCOURAGING YOURSELF since criticizing yourself hasn't worked.

> **VASHTI MURPHY MCKENZIE** at the Women of Power Summit, 2016; pioneer female bishop, African Methodist Episcopal Church; author

[I CHOSE LIFE in the streets] because in that space I felt accepted. . . . I was around other broken, fragile young males and we banded together around our brokenness.

> **SHAKA SENGHOR** on *Super Soul Sunday*; author of *Writing My Wrongs: Life, Death, and Redemption in an American Prison* (2016), entrepreneur, speaker, consultant

THERE IS NO greater battle in life than the battle between the parts of you that want to be healed and the parts of you that are comfortable and content being broken.

IYANLA VANZANT/Rhonda Harris on *Super Soul Sunday*;
life coach; author of *Trust* (2015), *Peace from Broken Pieces* (2010), and *Tapping the Power Within* (1992)

IF THERE'S NO enemy within you, you can beat the world.

DARNELL SUPERCHEF FERGUSON on *TMZ Live*, 2021;
award-winning chef, creator of urban eclectic cuisine, entrepreneur, philanthropist

TO GROW UP in the closet is to grow up as someone else. Detangling the presented self from the authentic self, while unlearning the miseducation, is an ongoing process.

ELZIE LEE "LZ" GRANDERSON in the *Los Angeles Times*, 2021;
columnist for CNN and the *Los Angeles Times*;
co-host, *SportsNation*, ESPN

BEING YOURSELF CAN be a revolutionary act. And in a world that wants us to whisper, I choose to yell.

LUVVIE AJAYI JONES in a January 2018 TED Talk;
author of *Professional Troublemaker: The Fear-Fighter Manual* (2021); host, *Professional Troublemaker* podcast

PEOPLE WHO ARE genuinely themselves are the most powerful people.

> RYAN RUSSELL on "Finding Free," The Undefeated/
> Andscape's ESPN *Black History Always* series;
> former NFL wide receiver

I DON'T HAVE to be what you want me to be. I'm free to be and think what I want to think.

> MUHAMMAD ALI (1942–2016) after winning the
> world title, 1964;
> three-time heavyweight boxing champion, philan-
> thropist, social justice hero, author of *The Soul of a
> Butterfly* (2003) and *The Greatest* (1975)

I LIKE WHO I am, I like how I look, and I love repre-senting the beautiful dark women out there. For me, it's perfect. I wouldn't want it any other way. . . . I've never been like anybody else in my life, and I'm not going to start now.

> SERENA WILLIAMS in *British Vogue*, November 2020;
> winner of twenty-three WTA Grand Slam titles,
> author of *My Life: Queen of the Court* (2009), social
> justice advocate

I FANTASIZED ALL the time about having a different life. And that manifested in creating characters and worlds and scenarios. I've definitely let my imagination run free.

ISSA RAE/Jo-Issa Rae Diop in *Essence*, April 2019;
actor, writer, producer, author of *The Misadventures of Awkward Black Girl* (2011)

[*BLACK PANTHER*] BROUGHT me closer to my roots. This movie took me to the continent of Africa, which is somewhere I wanted to go since my mom and dad sat me down and told me I was Black. . . . I hope to make movies that'll challenge me as an artist and as a person.

RYAN COOGLER in an NPR interview, 2018;
award-winning film director, screenwriter, producer

ONE OF THE preparations that I do always whenever I perform is I say a mantra to myself, which is "I'm the daughter of Black writers. We're descended from freedom fighters who broke through chains and changed the world."

AMANDA GORMAN on a television interview,
Inauguration Day, 2021;
U.S. Youth Poet Laureate (2017); author of *The Hill We Climb* (2021) and *Change Sings* (2021);
curator, Writing Change, Estèe Lauder literacy initiative

KNOWLEDGE OF ONE'S identity, one's self, community, nation, religion, and God, is the true meaning of resurrection, while ignorance of it signifies hell.

> ELIJAH MUHAMMAD (1897–1975) in *Message to the Black Man* (1965); leader, Nation of Islam

ALL OF US [Black folks] live in slightly different worlds, but crucial to the shaping of all our experiences and attitudes have been the values of the white American mainstream . . . , the anger that Malcolm X and others expressed about the white system's injustices, and the daily battles to survive and thrive in the space in between.

> NELSON GEORGE in *Buppies, B-Boys, Baps & Bohos* (1992); music and culture critic, award-winning writer, columnist, author of *The Darkest Hearts* (2020)

CHICAGO BLACKNESS GAVE me understanding, awareness, street sense and a rhythm.

> COMMON/Lonnie Rashid Lynn Jr. in *Ebony*, July 2016; rapper, actor, social justice advocate, author of *One Day It'll All Make Sense* (2011)

I AM A man who perceives life a certain way, a man who rejects . . . anything that will not give people room for dissent.

HARRY BELAFONTE
singer, actor, social justice advocate, author of *My Song* (2011)

BLACK CULTURE ALLOWED us to define ourselves to the world and to change America in ways both subtle and profound.

HENRY LOUIS GATES JR. on *Black America Since MLK: And Still I Rise* (2016); host, *Finding Your Roots*; author; director, Hutchins Center for African & African American Research, Harvard University

I'M A PRISONER of hope. I've been doing activist work since I was a teenager.

MARC LAMONT HILL on *Politically Re-Active with W. Kamau Bell & Hari Kondabolu*, 2021; co-author of *Except for Palestine: The Limits of Progressive Politics* (2021); professor, Temple University

THERE IS POWER in identity. When we create the right kind of identity, we can say things to the world around us that they don't actually believe make sense. We can get them to do things that they don't think they can do.

> **BRYAN STEVENSON** in a March 2012 TED Talk;
> founder and executive director, Equal Justice Initiative;
> 2016 MacArthur Fellow; author of *Just Mercy* (2014)

THE LAUGHTER INSPIRED by satire opens up space to acknowledge kaleidoscopic Blackness—the multiple autonomous ways of being Black—that prevents psychic death, or being objectified and flattened.

> **DANIELLE FUENTES MORGAN** in *Laughing to Keep*
> *from Dying* (2020);
> professor of English, Santa Clara University

THERE IS NOTHING more powerful than a people, than a nation, steeped in its history.

> **LONNIE G. BUNCH**
> Secretary of the Smithsonian Institution; founding
> director, National Museum of African American
> History and Culture

IT MATTERS LESS what you acquire than what you endure to acquire it.

JOHN JORDAN "BUCK" O'NEIL JR. (1911–2006)
on the PBS documentary *Baseball* (1994);
co-founder, Negro Leagues Baseball Museum (1990)

I'M HERE FOR good. I'm here to stay. I'm not an overnight sensation. . . . I'm going to be making films.

SPIKE LEE on *Entertainment Tonight*, 1986;
filmmaker, writer, director, author, winner of
Academy Award for Best Adapted Screenplay (2019)

STORYTELLING AND LITERATURE are more important than ever . . . [because] we need to explain to each other who we are and where we're going.

BARACK OBAMA in the *New York Times*, December 2020;
president of the United States (2009–17); author of
A Promised Land (2020)

POETRY IS A witness for life, so has to be right in the thick of it.

RITA DOVE on *Charlie Rose*, 1993;
U.S. Poet Laureate (1993–95), winner of Pulitzer
Prize for Poetry (1983), author, professor

I THINK THERE has to be more literature in the world that helps people navigate this world, navigate their own lives. Because life is hard and it's long.

TARANA BURKE in *Marie Claire*, 2021; author of *Unbound* (2021), *Time* Person of the Year (2017), founder, MeToo movement (2006)

SO WHO EXACTLY am I? Who do I love? What drives me? How does being a dark-skinned woman affect me as I move through life? None of it is explored. If you push writers to explore it. . . . They're going to take the parts of you that they feel they already know. They want the fantasy of what they feel they know about you. They don't want *you*.

VIOLA DAVIS in the *New York Times Magazine*, December 2020; Oscar, Tony, and Emmy Award–winning actor

FOR TOO LONG, powerful people have expected the people they have mistreated and marginalized to sacrifice themselves to make things whole. The burden of working for racial justice is laid on the very people bearing the brunt of the injustice, and not the powerful people who maintain it. I say to you: I refuse.

NIKOLE HANNAH-JONES in statement declining tenure at the University of North Carolina, 2021; author of *The 1619 Project: A New Origin Story* (2021), winner of Pulitzer Prize for Commentary (2020), 2017 MacArthur Fellow

IF I DIDN'T define myself for myself, I would be crunched into other people's fantasies for me and eaten alive.

AUDRE LORDE (1934–1992) in *Sister Outsider* (1984); Black, lesbian, mother, warrior, poet

GETTING TO DEFINE oneself can be the ultimate victory. But to fully appreciate that win, we first have to acknowledge the limitations we have placed on ourselves.

GWEN IFILL (1955–2016) in a *Washington Post* book review, 2011; moderator and managing editor, *Washington Week in Review*; co-anchor and managing editor, *PBS NewsHour*; author of *The Breakthrough* (2009)

WHEN I DISCOVER who I am, I'll be free.

RALPH ELLISON (1913–1994) in *Invisible Man* (1952); author of *Going to the Territory* (1986) and *Shadow and Act* (1964), National Book Award winner (1953)

MY BODY WENT to death row, but my mind never did.

ANTHONY RAY HINTON on *Soul of a Nation*, April 2021; twenty-eight years on death row in Alabama before exoneration with no compensation, author of *The Sun Does Shine* (2018)

WHEN YOU'RE CREATING your own shit . . . even the sky ain't the limit.

MILES DAVIS (1926–1991) in *Miles: The Autobiography* (1989); innovative musician, trumpet player, composer

I WRITE FROM my knowledge, not my lack, my strength, not my weakness. . . . I am interested in being understood, not admired. I wish to celebrate and not be celebrated.

LUCILLE CLIFTON (1936–2010) in *Black Women Writers 1950–1980* (1984); poet, author, Maryland Poet Laureate (1979–85)

WE SPEND SO much time hiding ourselves and trying to be something we're not. Or trying to make sure that nobody knows we're this person. And the minute you say, "This is who I am," it's so much better.

SHONDA RHIMES on *Super Soul Sunday*; television writer and producer, author of *Year of Yes* (2015)

THE MORE YOU invest in yourself as a celebrity, the less of yourself you own.

DAVE CHAPPELLE on *My Next Guest Needs No Introduction with David Letterman*, 2020; comedian, actor, winner of Mark Twain Prize for American Humor (2019)

WHEN YOU'RE OVERWEIGHT, your body becomes a matter of public record. . . . People are quick to offer you statistics and information about the dangers of obesity as if you are not only fat, but also incredibly stupid. . . . They forget that you are a person. You are a body, nothing more.

ROXANE GAY in *Hunger: A Memoir of (My) Body* (2017); contributing opinion writer for the *New York Times*; author of *Bad Feminist* (2014)

[IT'S] DANGEROUS TO allow other people to determine how you're going to feel about yourself.

WILL SMITH in a Holmes Place interview, 2016; rapper, producer, winner of Academy Award for Best Actor (2022)

I AM NO more interested in having Black people police my behavior than I am in having white people tell me what to do.

JANET CHEATHAM BELL author of *The Time and Place That Gave Me Life* (2007), curator of this collection

YOU HAVE TO know that your real home is within.

QUINCY JONES in *Q: The Autobiography of Quincy Jones* (2001); record producer, musician, songwriter, composer, arranger, author, film and television producer, twenty-eight-time Grammy Award winner

IN SEARCH OF my mother's garden, I found my own.

> **ALICE WALKER** in *In Search of Our Mothers' Gardens* (1983);
> author, poet, winner of Pulitzer Prize for Fiction
> (1983, *The Color Purple*)

WITHOUT HAVING THE wish to show "them," I developed a fierce desire to show *myself.* I wanted to vindicate every ability I had. I wanted to acquire new abilities. I wanted to prove that I, as an individual deserved a place in the world.

> **PAUL R. WILLIAMS** (1894–1980) on the PBS documentary *Hollywood's Architect* (2020);
> fellow, American Institute of Architects

IT ISN'T A calamity to die with dreams unfulfilled, but it is certainly a calamity not to dream.

> **BENJAMIN E. MAYS** (1894–1984) in *Born to Rebel* (1971);
> president, Morehouse College (1940–67); author

IF YOU DON'T dream, you might as well be dead.

> **GEORGE FOREMAN**
> entrepreneur, author, former heavyweight
> boxing champion

OVER THE YEARS I've been attacked from many different quarters for various political stands I've taken. That's to be expected. Welcomed, in fact, when you stand up for justice and try to tell the truth.

STOKELY CARMICHAEL/KWAME TURE (1941–1998)
in *Ready for Revolution: The Life and Struggles of Stokely Carmichael (Kwame Ture)* with Ekwueme Michael Thelwell (2003);
chair, SNCC (1966–67); founder, Lowndes County Black Panther Party

A LOT OF my critics would say, "All Al Sharpton wants is publicity." That's exactly what I want. People don't come to me to keep a secret; they come to me because they want me to make it a public issue. . . . If you can't make it a public issue, you'll never get change.

AL SHARPTON on the PBS documentary *The Black Church: This Is Our Story, This Is Our Song* (2021);
author of *Rise Up: Confronting a Country at the Crossroads* (2020);
founder, National Action Network

I WOULD NOT exchange my color for all the wealth in the world, for had I been born white, I might not have been able to do all I have done.

MARY MCLEOD BETHUNE (1875–1955)
founder, Bethune-Cookman College; advisor to President Franklin Roosevelt; founder, National Council of Negro Women (1935)

THERE IS NO future in any job, the future is in you.

DENNIS KIMBRO in *Think and Grow Rich: A Black Choice* (1991); educator, entrepreneur

LIKE WHAT YOU do, and then you will do your best.

KATHERINE JOHNSON (1918–2020) NASA mathematician and computer scientist, recipient of Presidential Medal of Freedom (2015), story depicted in film *Hidden Figures* (2016)

AIN'T NOTHING LIKE knowing who you are and what you're here to do. It's like having a fire inside that no one can extinguish. I've been in absolute awe in realizing I'm just getting started. I'm conditioning [and] preparing for the challenges ahead.

ANGELICA ROSS in an April 2021 tweet; founder and CEO, TransTech Social Enterprises; actor; social justice advocate

I WANT TO be strategic about the movies that I make and the roles that I play because you're immortalized forever once you get in front of that camera.

MICHAEL B. JORDAN on *Super Soul Sunday*; actor, director, producer, social justice advocate, *Time* 100 Most Influential (2020)

WHEN I READ a script: either my skin tingles or my stomach churns. When it tingles, I take it, and when my stomach churns, there's no way I could possibly do it. No way.

CICELY TYSON (1924–2021)
actor, author of *Just As I Am* (2021), Television
Academy Hall of Fame honoree (2020), recipient of
Presidential Medal of Freedom (2016), Tony Award
winner (2014), Emmy Award winner (1994, 1974)

I DON'T SING a song unless I feel it. The song don't tug at my heart, I pass on it. I have to believe in what I'm doing.

RAY CHARLES/Ray Charles Robinson (1930–2004);
singer, pianist, composer, Grammy Lifetime Achievement Award winner (1987)

NOBODY KNOWS YOU better than you. Only you know what resonates with you. And you know when there's an opportunity for you if it *feels* right.

ALICIA KEYS/Alicia Augello-Cook Dean on *Super Soul Sunday*;
musical artist, composer, actor, author of *More Myself:
A Journey* (2020)

EVERY SPECIAL I'VE done, at some point people go
BOO! That's how I like it. I like the audience to be slightly
appalled every now and then.

> CHRIS ROCK on *Right to Offend: The Black Comedy*
> *Revolution* (2022);
> comedian, actor, producer

I DO WHAT pleases me. I do the music I like. I don't know
if it's going to be English or French or some African dia-
lect. Music is music; it's all about communication.

> ANGÉLIQUE KIDJO in the *Toronto Star*;
> Grammy Award–winning vocalist, songwriter, social
> justice advocate

THERE IS SOMETHING in every one of you that waits and
listens for the sound of the genuine in yourself. It is the
only true guide you will ever have. And, if you cannot hear
it, you will, all of your life, spend your days on the ends of
strings that somebody else pulls.

> HOWARD THURMAN (1900–1981)
> mystic; theologian; author; founder, Church for the
> Fellowship of All Peoples

A LIFE IS not important, except for the impact it has on other lives.

JACKIE ROBINSON (1919–1972)
professional baseball player, social justice advocate

THE THING THAT makes you exceptional . . . is inevitably that which must also make you lonely.

LORRAINE HANSBERRY (1930–1965)
playwright, *A Raisin in the Sun* (1959)

I KNOW THAT everything that has happened *to* me has happened *for* me based on the intentions I've set for myself.

OPRAH WINFREY on *Super Soul Sunday*, 2016;
chief creative officer, OWN television

I'M NOT DOING anything different than what those old white men . . . are doing with their fantasy stories. They're interjecting their white dude ethics and aesthetics into what they write, and I'm doing the same thing with my fiction. The only difference is that our society is configured to see one of those things as perfectly normal, and the other as pathology.

N. K. JEMISIN
author of the *Broken Earth* trilogy, Hugo Award
winner (2016, 2017, 2018), *Time* 100 Most Influential
(2021), 2020 MacArthur Fellow

I'D RATHER PLAY a maid than be one.

HATTIE MCDANIEL (1893–1952)
winner of Academy Award for Best Actress in a
Supporting Role (1939)

AS AFRICAN AMERICANS, we find that our self-esteem comes under daily and rigorous assault. Many of us overspend to . . . fend off feelings of rejection, anger, and depression.

GLINDA BRIDGFORTH
author of *Girl, Get Your Money Straight* (2002);
founder, Bridgforth Financial Management Group

Early lessons stay with us and rob us of our feelings of belonging and security. . . . When we feel too hurt or afraid to let ourselves out, it becomes impossible to let others in.

> BRENDA WADE in *The Daily Word*, January/February 2021;
> psychologist, relationship expert, author of
> *Power Choices* (2005)

As a Black person I do sometimes find myself in my own bigotry, so I'm just learning to decolonize my mind around a lot of shit that I've been taught for so long. . . . I feel like we tend to box ourselves and fight for things that affect us directly, and with intersections of oppression I have learned that I'm connected to every fucked up thing that happens in the world regardless of if I want to see it that way or not.

> Chrishaun "CECE" MCDONALD in *HuffPost*, 2015;
> social justice advocate, charged with murder for
> defending herself (2011)

TRANS AND NON-BINARY issues are so incredibly important right now because trans liberation is integral to the
liberation of everyone. . . . What is more radical than living
in the fullness of your truth and inviting others to do the
same?

> JANAYA FUTURE KHAN in *Vogue*, November 2018;
> storyteller; organizer; movement strategist;
> co-founder, Black Lives Matter, Toronto

EVERY PERSON I look at is a reflection of my own mind.
What am I resisting now? What am I pushing away? What
do I not want to look at? What do I want to close off to?
Every time I open the door, I grow.

> SPRING WASHAM in *A Fierce Heart: Finding Strength,*
> *Courage, and Wisdom in Any Moment* (2019);
> co-founder, East Bay Meditation Center

I COULD NOT have fought against the discrimination of
apartheid and not also fight against the discrimination
that homosexuals endure, even in our churches and faith
groups.

> DESMOND MPILO TUTU (1931–2021) in *God Is Not a*
> *Christian* (2011);
> Anglican cleric and theologian, Nobel Peace Prize
> winner (1984)

THE CULTURAL EMPHASIS on endless consumption deflects attention from spiritual hunger.

BELL HOOKS/Gloria Watkins (1952–2021) in *All About Love: New Visions* (2000); author; professor; feminist theorist; founder, bell hooks Institute

IF WE DON'T exercise our freedom to create and to demand a wide range of life-enhancing returns for our labor, we're captives of a system with no center—moral, ethical, aesthetic—except production of wealth.

JOHN EDGAR WIDEMAN in introduction to *Ready for Revolution: The Life and Struggles of Stokely Carmichael* (*Kwame Ture*) with Ekwueme Michael Thelwell (2003); essayist, professor, award-winning novelist

I CANNOT GIVE you a sense of the importance of your life. I can confirm it, . . . but I cannot make it so for you. That you must do for yourself.

ANNE WORTHAM in *A World of Ideas* by Bill Moyers (1989); author of *The Other Side of Racism* (1981); professor of sociology, Illinois State University

WE MUST BELIEVE in ourselves enough to take a chance, not wait for a chance.

JANET CHEATHAM BELL in *Victory of the Spirit*
(1996, 2011);
author of *The Time and Place That Gave Me Life*
(2007), curator of this collection

WHATEVER WE BELIEVE about ourselves and our ability comes true for us.

SUSAN L. TAYLOR in *Essence*, August 1991;
editor-in-chief, *Essence* (1981–2000); author of
Lessons in Living (1995)

YOUR WORLD IS as big as you make it.

GEORGIA DOUGLAS JOHNSON (1880–1966)
poet, playwright, author of *The Heart of a Woman* (1918)

I FIRMLY BELIEVE that [with childhood years spent in the West Indies, Harry Belafonte and I] had the opportunity to arrive at the formation of a sense of ourselves without having it fucked with by racism as it existed in the United States.

SIDNEY POITIER (1927–2022) in "Belafonte's Balancing Act," the *New Yorker*, 1996;
author, director, and award-winning actor

THE BIGGEST ADVENTURE you can ever take is to live the life of your dreams.

OPRAH WINFREY in *Thought for Today* newsletter,
January 29, 2021;
chief creative officer, OWN television

FAULTS ARE LIKE a hill: You stand on top of your own and talk about those of other people.

HAUSA PROVERB

IT TOOK ME a hundred years to figure out I can't change the world. I can only change [myself]. And honey, that ain't easy either.

A. ELIZABETH DELANY (1891–1995) in *Having Our
Say: The Delany Sisters' First 100 Years* (1993)

I'VE GOT A great responsibility. . . . I wanted to be an inspiration for others—young Black men and women. . . . I wanted to see this as a way of opening the eyes of those who may have some bias, some reason not to hire someone because of their race.

WAYNE EMBRY on *The Jump*, ESPN, February 2021;
Basketball Hall of Fame inductee (1999); NBA general
manager, Milwaukee Bucks (1972–79)

YOUNG ATHLETES NEED to see people who are not going to be controlled by the system.

> **DOMINIQUE DAWES** on *Soul of a Nation*, 2021;
> retired gymnast, winner of four Olympic medals, U.S.
> Olympic Hall of Fame inductee (2008)

I THINK WE [NBA players] opened the doors for a lot of athletes to feel more comfortable and confident in speaking on issues.

> **CARMELO ANTHONY** on *Soul of a Nation*, 2021;
> ten-time NBA All-Star; member, Los Angeles Lakers;
> social justice advocate

ALL THAT YOU touch,
You Change
All that you Change,
Changes you.

> **OCTAVIA E. BUTLER** (1947–2006) in *Parable of the*
> *Sower* (1993);
> award-winning fantasy writer, 1995 MacArthur Fellow

As LONG AS you're here, you're here to do something. When I have done what He put me here to do, then He'll take me away.

CICELY TYSON (1924–2021)
actor, author of *Just As I Am* (2021), Television Academy Hall of Fame honoree (2020), recipient of Presidential Medal of Freedom (2016), Tony Award winner (2014), Emmy Award winner (1994, 1974)

As HUMAN BEINGS everybody has a natural gift and a natural passion. . . . For me to make art, I had to reflect on reality. As my life changed and the reality of what I was living changed, I had to change what fueled the art.

NIPSEY HUSSLE/Ermias Asghedom (1985–2019) on
MVMNT TV, March 2018;
rapper, social justice advocate

MY GIFTS COME from the places I'm the most wounded, and my joy comes from alleviating the suffering I feel in my own heart.

SPRING WASHAM in *A Fierce Heart: Finding Strength, Courage, and Wisdom in Any Moment* (2019);
co-founder, East Bay Meditation Center

THE GOAL IS not to be successful and famous. . . . We have a responsibility to push the conversation forward until we're all equal . . . in this place. Because until everyone's free, no one's free, and that's just a fact.

> **JAY-Z**/Shawn Carter in the *New York Times Style
> Magazine*, 2017;
> rapper, songwriter, entrepreneur, record producer

LEARNING HOW TO love myself in a world where who and what you represent is reviled took me a long time. And it's not lost on me that as a fifty-year-old Black gay man, I'm a part of the first generation who gets to live out loud and proud!

> **BILLY PORTER** on *TIME100*, 2020;
> Emmy and Tony Award–winning actor and singer

I'M SICK OF being an activist just because I'm fat and Black. I want to be an activist because I'm intelligent, because I care about issues, and because my music is good, because I wanna help the world.

> **LIZZO**/Melissa Viviane Jefferson on *My Next Guest
> Needs No Introduction with David Letterman*;
> musician, Grammy Award winner, *Time* Entertainer
> of the Year (2019)

WHEN SOMEONE IS cruel or acts like a bully, you don't stoop to their level. No. Our motto is, "When they go low, we go high."

MICHELLE OBAMA at the 2012 Democratic
National Convention;
First Lady of the United States (2009–17), author of
Becoming (2018)

[BIASES ARE] THE thoughts and feelings we have about social groups that can affect our decision-making and our actions even when we're not aware of it. . . . We're all susceptible to bias. . . . And it is triggered by our situation, and we can manage bias by managing those situations.

JENNIFER EBERHARDT at Palo Alto Reads, December 2020;
author of *Biased: Uncovering the Hidden Prejudice That
Shapes What We See, Think, and Do* (2019); professor of
psychology, Stanford University; 2014 MacArthur Fellow

I BELIEVE THAT each of us is more than the worst thing we've ever done. . . . And because of that, there's this basic human dignity that must be respected by law.

BRYAN STEVENSON at a 2012 TED Talk;
founder and executive director, Equal Justice Initiative;
2016 MacArthur Fellow; author of *Just Mercy* (2014)

EVEN OUR WORST decisions don't separate us from the circle of humanity.

WES MOORE on *Super Soul Sunday*;
author of *The Work* (2014) and *The Other Wes Moore: One Name, Two Fates* (2010); Rhodes Scholar

HOW DO [FORMER prisoners] re-emerge into a society that is so unforgiving?

SHAKA SENGHOR on *Super Soul Sunday*;
author of *Writing My Wrongs: Life, Death, and Redemption in an American Prison* (2016), entrepreneur, speaker, consultant

THERE'S ALWAYS LIGHT, if only we are brave enough to see it; if only we're brave enough to be it.

AMANDA GORMAN on *Amanda Gorman: Brave Enough with Robin Roberts*;
curator, Writing Change, Estèe Lauder literacy initiative; author of *The Hill We Climb* (2021) and *Change Sings* (2021), U.S. Youth Poet Laureate (2017)

WOMEN
OVERCOMING HANDICAPS

Colored women are the only group in this country to have two heavy handicaps to overcome. . . .

MARY CHURCH TERRELL

NEXT TO GOD we are indebted to women, first for life itself, and then for making it worth living.

MARY MCLEOD BETHUNE (1875–1955)
founder, Bethune-Cookman College; advisor to
President Franklin Roosevelt; founder, National
Council of Negro Women (1935)

THAT LITTLE MAN says women can't have the same rights as men 'cause Christ wasn't a woman! Where did your Christ come from? Where did your Christ come from? From God and a woman! Man had nothing to do with him.

SOJOURNER TRUTH/Isabella Baumfree (1797–1883)
at the Women's Rights Convention, 1851

TELL US NO more of southern slavery; for with few exceptions . . . I consider our condition but little better than that. . . . Let our girls['] . . . natural taste and ingenuity be what they may; it is impossible for scarce an individual of them to rise above the condition of servants.

MARIA W. STEWART (1803–1879) in a speech to the
New England Anti-Slavery Society, Boston, 1832

COLORED WOMEN ARE the only group in this country to have two heavy handicaps to overcome; race as well as that of sex.

MARY CHURCH TERRELL (1863–1954)
co-founder, National Association of Colored Women
(1896); author of *A Colored Woman in a White World*
(1940); educator; social justice advocate

OUR WHITE WOMEN friends were not willing to treat us on a plane of equality with themselves.

IDA B. WELLS-BARNETT (1862–1931) in *Crusade for Justice: The Autobiography of Ida B. Wells*, edited by Alfreda M. Duster (1970);
journalist; anti-lynching advocate; co-founder, NAACP

BEING A WOMAN, being a woman of color, has been a blessing for me. I wouldn't want to be anything else. But it is to walk a unique path and sit in that unique perch and travel this special journey. There are people who have a problem [with me] but it's their problem—it's not mine.

APRIL RYAN on Twitter's *HerStory* Q&A;
White House correspondent for *TheGrio*; political analyst, CNN; author

AMERICAN MONEY, AND our national romance with it, is the root of so many of our national evils. Too often America attempts to atone for racism through style and symbol rather than substance. We don't need America to put Black women on its money. We need America to put its money on Black women.

BRITTNEY COOPER in *Time*, January 27, 2021; professor of women's, gender, and sexuality studies, Rutgers University; author of *Eloquent Rage: A Black Feminist Discovers Her Superpower* (2018)

ONE OUGHT TO be against racism and sexism because they are wrong, not because one is Black or one is female.

ELEANOR HOLMES NORTON in *I Dream a World* (1989); lawyer; Washington, DC delegate to the U.S. House of Representatives (1991–)

BLACK WOMEN SIMULTANEOUSLY endure entrenched racism and sexism, the compounding effects of which often mean that their experiences of violence and racism are suppressed or overlooked.

JANAI NELSON president and director-counsel, NAACP Legal Defense and Educational Fund

IT'S OKAY SOMETIMES to even sit out the big competitions to focus on yourself because it shows how strong of a competitor or a person that you really are. . . . At the end of the day, we're not just athletes or entertainment. We're human too, and we have real emotions.

> SIMONE BILES in an interview at the 2020 Olympics;
> gymnast with over thirty world titles and Olympic
> medals, ESPY Best Female Athlete Award winner
> (2017), author of *Courage to Soar* (2016)

I FEEL LIKE my attitude wasn't that great because I don't really know how to cope with that pressure so that's the best that I could have done in this situation.

> NAOMI OSAKA in an interview at the 2020 Olympics;
> a top-ranked world WTA player, ESPY Best Female
> Athlete Award winner (2021), social justice advocate

CARING FOR OURSELVES is not self-indulgent; it is self-preservation.

> AUDRE LORDE (1934–1992)
> Black, lesbian, mother, warrior, poet, author of
> *Sister Outsider* (1984)

BLACK WOMEN, PARTICULARLY in corporate environments, feel like they don't belong, and it intensifies when people question their right to be in a place. . . . Being asked repetitive questions by the media exacerbates self-doubt. But many women feel it's easier to suffer in silence than to walk away.

> INGER BURNETT-ZEIGLER in the *Chicago Tribune*, 2021;
> author of *Nobody Knows the Trouble I've Seen: The Emotional Lives of Black Women* (2021); professor of psychiatry and behavioral sciences, Northwestern University

WHEN YOU'RE A Black woman, you seldom get to do what you just want to do; you always do what you have to do.

> DOROTHY I. HEIGHT (1912–2010)
> president, National Council of Negro Women
> (1958–90)

THROUGHOUT THE SOCIAL history of Black women, children are more important than marriage in determining the woman's domestic role.

> PAULA GIDDINGS in *When and Where I Enter* (1984);
> author; editor; journalist; professor emerita, Smith College

MOTHERHOOD IS A glorious gift, but do not define yourself solely by motherhood. Be a full person. Your child will benefit from that.

> CHIMAMANDA NGOZI ADICHIE in *Dear Ijeawele, or A Feminist Manifesto in Fifteen Suggestions* (2017); award-winning author, 2008 MacArthur Fellow

[THIS IS] A country that regards its women as its monsters, celebrating wherever possible the predatory coquette and carnivorous mother.

> TONI CADE BAMBARA (1939–1995) in *The Black Woman* (1970); writer, teacher, filmmaker, social justice advocate

IF WE WANT to avoid the murders of Black trans women, then we have to invest in the lives of Black trans women.

> ALICIA GARZA in *Vanity Fair*, November 2020; author of *The Purpose of Power* (2020); co-founder, Black Lives Matter (2013)

[I]T'S RIDICULOUS THAT some people think the simple phrase "Protect Black women" is controversial. We deserve to be protected as human beings. And we are entitled to our anger about a laundry list of mistreatment and neglect that we suffer.

> **MEGAN THEE STALLION**/Megan Jovon Ruth Pete in
> the *New York Times*, October 2020;
> rapper, entrepreneur, philanthropist

WE ALL MUST fight against the unnecessary barriers placed on trans women and girls by lawmakers and those who co-opt the feminist label in the name of division and hatred.

> **WANDA SYKES** in a March 2021 tweet;
> comic, producer, actor, award-winning writer, author
> of *Yeah, I Said It* (2004)

[T]O SPEAK OUT provoked violence; to remain silent encouraged death. It was a dilemma not at all new to people of color, or women.

> **ALICE WALKER** in *The Way Forward Is with a Broken*
> *Heart* (2000);
> author, poet, winner of Pulitzer Prize for Fiction
> (1983, *The Color Purple*)

YOUR SILENCE WILL not protect you.

AUDRE LORDE (1934–1992)
Black, lesbian, mother, warrior, poet, author of
Sister Outsider (1984)

BLACK WOMEN ARE not here to compete or fight with you, brothers. If we have hang-ups about being male or female, we're not going to be able to use our talents to liberate all of our Black people.

SHIRLEY CHISHOLM (1924–2005)
U.S. representative (1969–83), educator, author of
Unbought and Unbossed (1970)

BLACK WOMEN ARE up to four times more likely to die from complications related to giving birth. That this particular disparity exists . . . in the United States, one of the wealthiest countries in the world, is unconscionable.

ILHAN OMAR in *Vanity Fair*, September 2020;
author of *This Is What America Looks Like* (2020), U.S.
representative (2019–)

I AM HEARTBROKEN . . . for the mother of a nonviable pregnancy who is now forced to bring that pregnancy to term . . . for the health care workers who can no longer help them without risking jail time.

MICHELLE OBAMA in response to the decision
overturning *Roe v. Wade*;
First Lady of the United States (2009–17), author of
Becoming (2018)

WHEN YOU GRAB hold to a woman, you got something there. You got a whole world there. You got a way of life kicking up under your hand. That woman take and make you feel like something.

AUGUST WILSON (1945–2005) in *Joe Turner's Come
and Gone* (1988);
Tony Award– and Pulitzer Prize–winning playwright

SHE IS A friend of my mind. She gather me, man. The pieces I am, she gather them and give them back to me in all the right order. It's good, you know, when you got a woman who is a friend of your mind.

TONI MORRISON (1931–2019) in *Beloved* (1987);
author, professor, recipient of Presidential Medal of
Freedom (2012), winner of Nobel Prize in Literature
(1993) and Pulitzer Prize for Fiction (1988)

ONLY THE BLACK woman can say, "When and where I enter . . . then and there the whole race enters with me."

ANNA JULIA COOPER (1858–1964) in
A Voice from the South (1892);
author, scholar, educator, sociologist, social
justice advocate

WE BLACK WOMEN are the single group in the West intact. And anybody can see we're pretty shaky. We are, however (all praises), the only group that derives its identity from itself.

NIKKI GIOVANNI
poet; author; social justice advocate; distinguished
professor of English, Virginia Tech University

I WANT . . . TO let women know that in spite of what others say you cannot do, you can do [whatever you want].

JONNETTA PATTON on *Behind Every Man*;
entrepreneur, Usher's mother and manager

GIRLS ARE CAPABLE of doing everything men are capable of doing. Sometimes they have more imagination than men.

KATHERINE JOHNSON (1918–2020)
NASA mathematician and computer scientist,
recipient of Presidential Medal of Freedom (2015),
story depicted in *Hidden Figures* (2016)

NOW THAT WE [Black women] know our power, we have to use it to influence those around us.

> **VALERIE JARRETT** on *Black Women OWN the Conversation*;
> author of *Finding My Voice* (2019), senior advisor to
> President Barack Obama

FEMINISM AND FEMININITY are not mutually exclusive. It is misogynistic to suggest that they are.

> **CHIMAMANDA NGOZI ADICHIE** in *Dear Ijeawele, or A
> Feminist Manifesto in Fifteen Suggestions* (2017);
> award-winning author, 2008 MacArthur Fellow

SISTERS HAVE TAUGHT me that we should listen to the poetry within, capture and express our inner beauty as part of our political and social being.

> **MANNING MARABLE** (1950–2011) in *Essence*, May 1991;
> social justice advocate, professor, author of *Malcolm
> X: A Life of Reinvention* (2011)

THAT MAN OVER there says that women need to be helped into carriages, and lifted over ditches, and to have the best place everywhere. Nobody ever helps me into carriages, or over mud puddles, or gives me any best place! And ain't I a woman?

> **SOJOURNER TRUTH**/Isabella Baumfree (1797–1883)
> at the Women's Rights Convention, 1851

WE, THE BLACK women of today, must accept the full weight of a legacy wrought in blood by our mothers in chains . . . as heirs to a tradition of supreme perseverance and heroic resistance.

ANGELA Y. DAVIS
professor emerita, University of California, Santa
Cruz; social justice advocate; author of *Freedom Is a
Constant Struggle* (2015)

I AM A Black woman
the music of my song
some sweet arpeggio of tears
is written in a minor key

MARI EVANS (1923–2017) in *I Am a Black Woman* (1970);
poet, musician, educator, author

IT'S A FABULOUS thing to be a Black woman!

NIKKI GIOVANNI on *Politically Re-Active with W.
Kamau Bell & Hari Kondabolu*;
poet; author; social justice advocate; distinguished
professor of English, Virginia Tech University

MEN
FINDING THAT BALANCE

... And a man's balance depends on the weight
he carries between his legs.

JAMES BALDWIN

BLACK MALES HAVE long intrigued the Western imagination. . . . The Black male . . . has been represented in Western culture as the central enigma of a humanity wrapped in the darkest and deepest subliminal fantasies of Europe and America's collective cultural id.

> HENRY LOUIS GATES JR. in *Black Male: Represen-*
> *tations of Masculinity in Contemporary American Art*,
> Whitney Museum of American Art (1994);
> director, Hutchins Center for African & African
> American Research, Harvard University; host,
> *Finding Your Roots*

A MAN MUST defend himself, if only to demonstrate his fitness to defend anything else.

> FREDERICK DOUGLASS (1817–1895) in *Narrative of the*
> *Life of Frederick Douglass, an American Slave* (1845);
> enslaved until age nineteen, abolitionist, orator, author

WHEN I WALK down the street people don't see Stanford [University]; they don't see *doctor*. They see just another Black guy, and that puts me at the same level of risk as Jacob Blake [shot in the back seven times by police]. So I have this same level of stress and anxiety about being in society. I see a cop in the rearview my palms get sweaty.

> LEROY SIMS in *Stanford* magazine, December 2020;
> senior vice president of medical affairs, NBA

MEN ARE NOT women, and a man's balance depends on the weight he carries between his legs.

> **JAMES BALDWIN** (1924–1987) in *No Name in the Street* (1972); essayist, novelist, playwright, social justice advocate

WITH THE BEST will and knowledge, no man can know women's wants as well as women themselves. To disfranchise women is deliberately to turn from knowledge and grope in darkness.

> **W. E. B. DU BOIS** (1868–1963) in *Darkwater* (1920); author; professor; co-founder, NAACP

THERE IS A great stir about colored men getting their rights but not a word about colored women; and if colored men get their rights and not colored women theirs, you see, colored men will be masters over the women.

> **SOJOURNER TRUTH**/Isabella Baumfree (1797–1883) at the Women's Rights Convention, 1851

IF MEN COULD become pregnant, abortion would be a sacrament.

> **FLORYNCE "FLO" KENNEDY** (1916–2000) lawyer, feminist, social justice advocate

IT REALLY IS about keeping women barefoot and pregnant! These insecure, patriarchal men who believe in things like "legitimate rape" . . . are terrified of competing with women and cravenly disguise their fear as "religious liberty."

JANET CHEATHAM BELL in "Choosing a Life in the
Dark Age," *Not All Poor People Are Black* (2015);
author of *The Time and Place That Gave Me Life*
(2007), curator of this collection

WOMEN SHOULD NOT be expected to make marriage-based changes that men are not expected to make.

CHIMAMANDA NGOZI ADICHIE in *Dear Ijeawele, or A
Feminist Manifesto in Fifteen Suggestions* (2017);
award-winning author, 2008 MacArthur Fellow

FOR MEN AND women to have equal power in society, men would have to cede some of the power that they hold. . . . People in power have to start to recognize that *equality* is not *oppression*.

ROXANE GAY on *The Women's Power Drop*, BBC Select, 2021;
contributing opinion writer for the *New York Times*,
author of *Bad Feminist* (2014)

SHE'S JUST USING him to keep from being by herself.
That's the worst use of a man you can have.

> **AUGUST WILSON** (1945–2005) in *Joe Turner's Come
> and Gone* (1988);
> Tony Award– and Pulitzer Prize–winning playwright

THERE'S NOTHING MORE dangerous and destructive in a
household than a frustrated, oppressed Black man.

> **NATHAN MCCALL** in *Makes Me Wanna Holler* (1994);
> journalist, author

HIS CARE SUGGESTED a family relationship rather than a
man's laying claim.

> **TONI MORRISON** (1931–2019) in *Beloved* (1987);
> author, professor, recipient of Presidential Medal of
> Freedom (2012), winner of Nobel Prize in Literature
> (1993) and Pulitzer Prize for Fiction (1988)

A WOMAN CAN get teased for sounding like she's white,
but for a man it's more of a social sin. You're not quite
masculine. You're not tough.

> **JOHN MCWHORTER** in *Stanford* magazine,
> December 2020;
> cranky liberal Democrat, linguist, author, cultural critic

FATHERS AND SONS arrive at that relationship only by claiming that relationship: that is by paying for it. If the relationship of father to son could really be reduced to biology, the whole earth would blaze with the glory of fathers and sons.

JAMES BALDWIN (1924–1987) in *The Devil Finds Work* (1976); essayist, novelist, playwright, social justice advocate

I DIDN'T KNOW how to [create myself] and become a healthy and whole human being. It seemed that every Black man I witnessed attempting to create himself came through to the other side broken.

MYCHAL DENZEL SMITH in *Invisible Man, Got the Whole World Watching: A Young Black Man's Education* (2016); contributing writer for *The Nation*

WHEN A MAN wants something from another man, he knows he can't be disrespectful or insult him. But when it comes to women, that awareness goes away completely.

TARANA BURKE in *Street Roots*, 2018; author of *Unbound* (2021); *Time* Person of the Year (2017); founder, MeToo movement (2006)

VIOLENCE AGAINST WOMEN . . . happens because too many men treat all women as objects, which helps them to justify inflicting abuse against us when we choose to exercise our own free will.

> **MEGAN THEE STALLION**/Megan Jovon Ruth Pete in
> the *New York Times*, October 13, 2020;
> rapper, philanthropist, entrepreneur

[R]ICH AND POWERFUL men are indeed rich and power-ful, and they can shield themselves with the most talented and aggressive legal talent. . . . Society now takes a very different view of sexual harassment, exploitation, and assault than it did even a few years ago. The legal system takes a different view as well—but its ability to punish cold-case crimes is inherently limited.

> **EUGENE ROBINSON** in the *Washington Post*, July 2021;
> syndicated columnist and associate editor for the
> *Washington Post*; author of *Disintegration: The Splinter-*
> *ing of Black America* (2010); winner of Pulitzer Prize
> for Commentary (2009)

BAD JUDGMENT AND carelessness are not punishable by rape.

> **PEARL CLEAGE** in *Mad at Miles* (1990);
> playwright, social justice advocate, author

I HAVE INCREASINGLY found that many Black men just want better access to patriarchy. They don't actually want it dismantled.

JEMELE HILL in an October 2020 tweet;
sports journalist, social justice advocate

AND GOD SAID: Adam,
What hast thou done? . . .
And Adam,
With his head hung down,
Blamed it on the woman.

JAMES WELDON JOHNSON (1871–1938) in
God's Trombones (1927);
author, professor, poet, lyricist for
"Lift Every Voice and Sing"

WE PUT MEN in positions of power all the time because we trust them to take care of us. And when it's time, they often let us down.

LIZZO/Melissa Viviane Jefferson on *My Next Guest
Needs No Introduction with David Letterman*;
musician, Grammy Award winner, *Time* Entertainer
of the Year (2019)

IF YOU ARE wise and seek to make your house stable, love your wife fully and righteously. . . . Kindness and consideration will influence her better than force.

> **THE HUSIA**: *Sacred Wisdom of Ancient Egypt*,
> translated by **MAULANA KARENGA**;
> author, creator of Kwanzaa, Africana studies scholar

WHO'S RAISING BLACK men in this country? Black women. So, if Black men are not being very conscious of Black women, then it is our fault.

> **BERTHA KNOX GILKEY** (1949–2014)
> community organizer

SOMETIMES MOTHERS, SO conditioned to be all and do all, are complicit in diminishing the role of fathers.

> **CHIMAMANDA NGOZI ADICHIE** in *Dear Ijeawele, or A
> Feminist Manifesto in Fifteen Suggestions* (2017);
> award-winning author; 2008 MacArthur Fellow

MEDIA FASCINATION AROUND Black masculinity is almost always concentrated in three areas: sex, crime, and sports.

> **THELMA GOLDEN** in *Black Male: Representations of
> Masculinity in Contemporary American Art*, Whitney
> Museum of American Art (1994);
> director, Studio Museum

SOME PEOPLE SAY young Black men are an endangered species. But that's not true 'cause endangered species are protected by the government.

CHRIS ROCK on *Tamborine* (2018);
comedian, actor, producer

THERE'S AN INCREDIBLE amount of magic and feistiness in Black men that nobody has been able to wipe out. But everybody has tried.

TONI MORRISON (1931–2019)
author, professor, recipient of Presidential Medal of
Freedom (2012), winner of Nobel Prize in Literature
(1993) and Pulitzer Prize for Fiction (1988)

NOT THAT SUCCESS, for him, is sure, infallible.
But never has he been afraid to reach.
His lesions are legion.
But reaching is his rule.

GWENDOLYN BROOKS (1917–2000) in *Annie Allen* (1949);
winner of Pulitzer Prize for Poetry (1950), Illinois
Poet Laureate

CHILDREN
PREPARING THE FUTURE

Education is our passport to the future.

MALCOLM X

THE TRADITIONAL NUCLEAR family form of husband and wife and their children, with the husband in the work force and the wife-mother as full-time homemaker may . . . more accurately be perceived as a transitory human response to changing technology.

ANDREW BILLINGSLEY in *Climbing Jacob's Ladder* (1992);
sociologist; president, Morgan State University
(1975–84)

UNDERSTANDING WHAT PERMITS many single mothers to raise successful children may be every bit as important as understanding the power of paternal love.

ELLIS COSE
author of *Democracy, If We Can Keep It* (2020),
columnist and contributing editor for *Newsweek*

THE IDEA OF *family* is constantly shifting, so varied in its many shapes that the narrative of family is as unpredict-able as families themselves.

MARY HELEN WASHINGTON in *Memory of Kin* (1991);
author; professor of English, University of Maryland

EDUCATION IS AN important element in the struggle . . . to help our children and people rediscover their identity and thereby increase self-respect. Education is our passport to the future.

> MALCOLM X/el-Hajj Malik el-Shabazz (1925–1965) in "Statement of Basic Aims and Objectives," Organization of Afro-American Unity, 1964; National Representative of the Nation of Islam; founder, Organization of Afro-American Unity

FOR COLORED PEOPLE to acquire learning in this country makes tyrants quake and tremble on their sandy foundation.

> DAVID WALKER (1796–1830) in *Walker's Appeal, in Four Articles* (1829); abolitionist, writer

[THESE WOMEN] SCHOOL founders were collectively committed to education as a counteroffensive to racial degradation and an instrument of uplift for themselves and their race.

> AUDREY THOMAS MCCLUSKEY in *A Forgotten Sisterhood: Pioneering Black Women Educators and Activists in the Jim Crow South* (2014); professor emerita, Indiana University

EDUCATIONAL REFORM . . . [IS] focused on academic standards and content rather than on child development and relationship issues.

> **JAMES P. COMER** in *Maggie's American Dream* (1988);
> professor of child psychiatry; associate dean, Yale
> School of Medicine

FIX THE SCHOOLS without fixing the families and the community, and children will fail.

> **GEOFFREY CANADA**
> founder and president, Harlem Children's Zone;
> educator; author of *Fist Stick Knife Gun* (1995)

WE NEED TO stop punishing children because we don't like their parents.

> **MARIAN WRIGHT EDELMAN** in *The Measure of Our
> Success* (1992);
> founder and president emerita, Children's Defense
> Fund; author of *The State of America's Children* (2000)
> and *Families in Peril* (1987)

IT IS EASIER to build strong children than repair broken [adults].

> **FREDERICK DOUGLASS** (1817–1895)
> enslaved until age nineteen, abolitionist, orator, author

YOU CAN PAY for a student in two ways. You can pay for education now, or you can pay for incarceration later.

> MONIQUE DAVIS on *United Shades of America with W. Kamau Bell*, 2020; high school teacher

VIOLENCE IS BLACK children going to school for twelve years and receiving six years' worth of education.

> JULIAN BOND (1940–2015) in a 1976 speech; co-founder, SNCC; co-founder, Southern Poverty Law Center; author; essayist; poet; national chair, NAACP (1998–2009)

THE WOLVES ARE coming in the shape of [school] vouchers, dressed in sheep's clothing!

> WENDELL ANTHONY in *Newsweek*, November 1999; president, Detroit NAACP

VOUCHERS DON'T EDUCATE, they segregate.

> KWEISI MFUME in *Newsweek*, November 1999; CEO, NAACP (1996–2004); U.S. representative (1987–96, 2020–)

THE PRICE OF admission to the white race in America has been exacting. Costs . . . have included ethnic conflicts, class exploitation, police intimidation, humiliation by teachers, child abuse, lost self-esteem, and a general feeling of self-contempt. . . . The story of this racial victim is rarely told.

> **THANDEKA**/Sue Booker in *Learning to Be White:*
> *Money, Race, and God in America* (1999);
> scholar, theologian, ordained minister, journalist,
> author, television producer

WHITE CHILDREN NEED protection from all the verbal and nonverbal messages in our society telling them they are special—not simply because they are individual, unique, and precious humans, but because they are white.

> **IBRAM X. KENDI** in *How to Raise an Antiracist* (2022);
> director, Boston University Center for Antiracist
> Research; author of *How to Be an Antiracist* (2019);
> *Time* 100 Most Influential (2020)

EDUCATION CAN BE one of the most liberating forces in the world, but it can also be one of the most oppressive. Twelve years of segregated schooling teaches you some powerful lessons not featured in textbooks.

> **ROBERT L. GREEN** in *The Urban Challenge—*
> *Poverty and Race* (1977);
> professor emeritus, Michigan State University

PEOPLE WHO THINK education is expensive have never counted the cost of ignorance.

> **ANDREW YOUNG** in *An Easy Burden* (1996);
> mayor of Atlanta (1981–89), U.N. ambassador
> (1977–79), U.S. representative (1973–77), author

THE OMISSION OF Black, Indigenous, Brown, Asian, and Latinx history is not incidental. These exclusions distance people from their own heritage, their own lineage, and ultimately, their own sense of self. A whitewashed curriculum enforces the myth that there have never been scholars, thinkers, innovators, caregivers, iconoclasts, artists, and revolutionaries across these various identities.

> **ILYASAH SHABAZZ** in *Elle* magazine, February 2021;
> educator, co-author of *Growing Up X* (2002), social
> justice advocate

THE EMPLOYMENT AGENCY approach of most schools . . . does not emphasize the beauties, the absolute joy of learning.

> **AMIRI BARAKA/LEROI JONES** (1934–2014) in *The
> Autobiography of LeRoi Jones/Amiri Baraka* (1983);
> playwright, poet, essayist

[EDUCATION] IS SO workforce driven. . . . We're trained and not educated. We shortchange history, art, foreign language, overlooking the need to have fully educated people.

KAMAU BOBB on *United Shades of America with W. Kamau Bell*, 2021; founder and senior director, Constellations Center for Equity in Computing, Georgia Tech College of Computing

A CHOICE HAS been made. It is a deliberate choice. . . . Rather than good schools, we have been willing to build high-tech prisons. Rather than create jobs and invest in the communities that need it most, we have embarked on an unprecedented race to incarcerate that has left millions of Americans permanently locked up or locked out.

MICHELLE ALEXANDER in a University of Chicago lecture, 2013; author of *The New Jim Crow* (2010), lawyer, professor, social justice advocate

THE U.S. IS home to approximately 20% of all prisoners in the world even though it has only 4.4% of the world's population. A staggering 2.12 million people are in U.S. prisons instead of in the communities they call home.

MARK P. FANCHER in "Where Incarceration Isn't the Answer," *YES! The Better Ideas Issue*, Fall 2020; human rights attorney, writer

I HAVE A dream that my four little children will one day live in a nation where they will not be judged by the color of their skin, but by the content of their character.

MARTIN LUTHER KING JR. (1929–1968) at the
March on Washington for Jobs and Freedom, 1963;
Nobel Peace Prize winner (1964)

CHILDREN HAVE NEVER been very good at listening to their elders, but they have never failed to imitate them.

JAMES BALDWIN (1924–1987)
essayist, novelist, playwright, social justice advocate

YOU HAVE TO educate your children on the world as it exists today and how it got to that space, but my child doesn't need the same tools that I needed growing up. I needed certain tools to survive my area that my child doesn't need. They're growing up in a different environment. But also they have to know their history. Have a sense of what it took to get to this place. And have compassion for others.

JAY-Z/Shawn Carter in the *New York Times Style
Magazine*, 2017;
rapper, songwriter, entrepreneur, music producer

YOUR CHILDREN NEED your presence more than your presents.

JESSE JACKSON
candidate for U.S. president (1984, 1988); founder,
Rainbow/PUSH Coalition; author of *Keeping Hope
Alive* (2019) and *Legal Lynching* (1996)

MY CHILDREN ARE my teachers. . . . The children I got sent came in perfect, and I have to figure out how to grow and evolve so that I can support the truth of them.

KERRY WASHINGTON in *Marie Claire*, October 2018;
actor, producer

EACH LIFE HAS its own purpose, even the lives of our children, and that purpose is not dictated by [the parents'] needs.

TARANA BURKE in *Unbound* (2021);
Time Person of the Year (2017), founder, MeToo
movement (2006)

WHEN OUR CHILD comes home with . . . anything, it's our job as parents to listen to that, to give them the . . . best feedback that we can. And that doesn't change because sexuality is now involved in it.

DWYANE WADE on *The Ellen DeGeneres Show*;
retired three-time NBA champion; part owner, Utah Jazz

IN A CHILD'S eyes, a mother is a goddess. She can be glorious or terrible, benevolent or filled with wrath, but she commands love either way. I am convinced this is the greatest power in the universe.

N. K. JEMISIN in *The Hundred Thousand Kingdoms* (2010);
Time 100 Most Influential (2021), 2020 MacArthur
Fellow, Hugo Award winner (2016, 2017, 2018)

A CHILD WHO is to be successful is not reared exclusively on a bed of down.

AKAN PROVERB

CHILDREN ARE NOT ours
nor we theirs
they are future
we are past

NIKKI GIOVANNI
poet; author; social justice advocate; distinguished
professor of English, Virginia Tech University

[MY PARENTS] WERE comfortable with me exploring ideas that they were not proficient in. Some parents just aren't comfortable with that.

MAE JEMISON in the *Chicago Tribune*, April 1994;
astronaut, chemical engineer, physician, author of
Find Where the Wind Goes (2001)

AN ERROR MEANS a child needs help, not a reprimand or ridicule for doing something wrong.

> **MARVA COLLINS** (1936–2015)
> author of *Ordinary Children, Extraordinary Teachers* (1992) and *Marva Collins' Way* (1982); founder, Westside Preparatory School (1972)

I EARLY LEARNED that it is a hard matter to convert an individual by abusing [them].

> **BOOKER T. WASHINGTON** (1856–1915) in *Up from Slavery* (1901);
> co-founder and president, Tuskegee Institute

NO ONE RISES to low expectations.

> **LES BROWN**
> motivational speaker, author of *Live Your Dreams* (1992) and *It's Not Over Until You Win* (1997)

A PERSON IS a person through other persons.

> **BANTU PROVERB**

[IN THE FOSTER care system] there's nothing that's really yours except this trash bag [with your clothes], but if you give them a suitcase they can put their things in, they can feel like a traveler. If I'm able to do anything, I'm gonna try to figure out a way to make sure that kids don't feel like garbage.

TIFFANY HADDISH on *My Next Guest Needs No Introduction with David Letterman*; actor, comedian, author of *The Last Black Unicorn* (2017)

LOVE
WILLING SACRIFICES

The willingness to sacrifice is a necessary
dimension of loving practice.
BELL HOOKS

OF ALL WEAPONS, love is the most deadly and devastating, and few there be who dare trust their fate in its hands.

HOWARD THURMAN (1900–1981) in *Disciplines of the Spirit* (1963); mystic; theologian; author; founder, Church for the Fellowship of All Peoples

YOU CAN USE hatred as a weapon, but you cannot use hatred to defeat hate.

MARTIN LUTHER KING JR. (1929–1968) Nobel Peace Prize winner (1964)

WAR IS NOT the answer, for only love can conquer hate.

MARVIN GAYE (1939–1984) in "What's Going On" (1971); singer, songwriter, music producer

HATE IS REALLY just fear in a different octave.

MICHELE NORRIS on the CNN *First Ladies* documentary (2020); journalist; columnist for the *Washington Post*

You have to recognize that hatred often comes from a place of fear and pain. . . . One of the big themes of this white supremacist movement is the "browning" of America.

SARA SIDNER on *United Shades of America with W. Kamau Bell*, 2020; award-winning CNN news correspondent

Fear is imagination used for the wrong purpose.

OSHOKE PAMELA ABALU architect; co-founder, Love & Magic Company

Remember, to hate, to be violent, is demeaning. It means you're afraid of the other side of the coin—to love and be loved.

JAMES BALDWIN in *Artist on Fire* by William J. Weatherby (1989); essayist, novelist, playwright, social justice advocate

Hatred is infectious and cumulative—it begins with pejoratives about race and evolves into acts of unspeakable violence. We must do more than condemn. Our responsibility is to protect and defend. By word and deed.

STACEY ABRAMS in a March 21, 2021, tweet lawyer; entrepreneur; founder, Fair Fight; author of *Lead from the Outside* (2018)

MANY PEOPLE OF color . . . [cling] to festering old grudges, the better to foster communal solidarity. . . . But hate is hate. Disgust is almost always a damaging emotion, and contempt eats away at the soul, no matter who you are.

MICHELE NORRIS in *The Grace of Silence: A Memoir* (2009);
journalist; columnist for the *Washington Post*

PEOPLE WHO HURT other people have usually been hurt so badly themselves that all they know to do is hurt back.

TERRY MCMILLAN in *Disappearing Acts* (1989);
author of *Waiting to Exhale* (1992)

VIOLENCE AS A way of achieving racial justice is both impractical and immoral. It is impractical because it is a descending spiral ending in destruction for all. . . . Violence is immoral because it thrives on hatred rather than love.

MARTIN LUTHER KING JR. (1929–1968) in *Stride Toward Freedom* (1958);
Nobel Peace Prize winner (1964)

I THINK YOU realize how much you need to have people that you love. It's not as much about them loving you—it's about you needing to love people.

CHADWICK BOSEMAN (1976–2020) in *GQ*,
September 2014;
writer, director, award-winning actor

LOVE IS THE ability to extend yourself to others expecting nothing in return.

A. R. BERNARD on *Super Soul Sunday*;
founder and senior pastor, Christian Cultural Center

OUR LOVE IS a rock against the wind
not soft like silk and lace.

ETHERIDGE KNIGHT (1931–1991) in "A Love Poem"
from *Born of a Woman* (1980);
American Book Award winner for *The Essential Etheridge Knight* (1987), author of *Poems from Prison* (1968)

LOVE IS ALL that there is.

MICHAEL BERNARD BECKWITH on *Super Soul Sunday*;
founder, Agape International Spiritual Center

LOVE

THERE IS MORE to the Black experience in America than mourning, anger, and outrage. There's more to our humanity. [In "Bigger Love"] I was looking for the sound of love in what is a pretty scary time.

JOHN LEGEND/John Roger Stephens in *Variety*;
musical artist, performer, film and television producer, EGOT winner, social justice advocate

THE FOUNDATION OF my life is my spiritual life. I prayed to be one hundred percent guided by my soul.

INDIA.ARIE Simpson on *Super Soul Sunday*;
musical artist, songwriter, Grammy Award winner,
NAACP Image Award winner

SPIRITUALITY IS OUR human capacity to know and expe-rience God.

A. R. BERNARD on *Super Soul Sunday*;
founder and senior pastor, Christian Cultural Center

THE ONLY JUSTIFICATION for ever looking down on somebody is to pick them up.

JESSE JACKSON
candidate for U.S. president (1984, 1988); founder,
Rainbow/PUSH Coalition; author of *Keeping Hope
Alive* (2019) and *Legal Lynching* (1996)

WHEN YOU LOVE someone you love their journey.

ALICIA KEYS/Alicia Augello-Cook Dean on
Super Soul Sunday;
musical artist, composer, actor, author of *More Myself:*
A Journey (2020)

I HAVE A strong suspicion . . . that much that passes for constant love is a golded-up moment walking in its sleep.

ZORA NEALE HURSTON (1891–1960) in *Dust Tracks*
on a Road (1942);
folklorist, anthropologist, author of *Their Eyes Were*
Watching God (1937)

JUSTICE IS WHAT love looks like in public.

CORNEL WEST
professor, Harvard University; author of *Democracy*
Matters (2004); social justice advocate

NO PERSON IS your friend who demands your silence, or denies your right to grow.

ALICE WALKER in *In Search of Our Mothers'*
Gardens (1983);
author, poet, winner of Pulitzer Prize for Fiction
(1983, *The Color Purple*)

WHEN SOMEBODY SHOWS you who they are, believe them the first time.

MAYA ANGELOU (1928–2014)
poet, performer, author, social justice advocate

NOT EVERYBODY IS healthy enough to have a front-row seat in your life.

SUSAN L. TAYLOR in *In the Spirit* (1993);
editor-in-chief, *Essence* (1981–2000), author of
Lessons in Living (1995)

LOVE IS OR it ain't. Thin love ain't love at all.

TONI MORRISON (1931–2019) in *Beloved* (1987);
author, professor, recipient of Presidential Medal of
Freedom (2012), winner of Nobel Prize in Literature
(1993) and Pulitzer Prize for Fiction (1988)

LOVE CAMOUFLAGES ITSELF when it's under constant threat.

N. K. JEMISIN
author of *Broken Earth* trilogy, *Time* 100 Most Influential (2021), 2020 MacArthur Fellow, Hugo Award
winner (2016, 2017, 2018)

BEING BLACK [IS] not enough. It [takes] more than a community of skin color to make your love come down on you.

> ZORA NEALE HURSTON (1891–1960) in *Dust Tracks on a Road* (1942); folklorist, anthropologist, author of *Their Eyes Were Watching God* (1937)

IF OUR SOCIETY had a commonly held understanding of the meaning of love, the act of loving would not be so mystifying.

> BELL HOOKS/Gloria Watkins (1952–2021) in *All About Love: New Visions* (2000); author; professor; feminist theorist; founder, bell hooks Institute

IF THIS COUNTRY were not so mesmerized with sex, and focused more on the characteristics of non-erotic love, our success rate with erotic pairings might improve. We might also have less incest and pedophilia.

> JANET CHEATHAM BELL in *Victory of the Spirit* (1996, 2011); author of *The Time and Place That Gave Me Life* (2007), curator of this collection

HABIT IS HEAVEN'S own redress: it takes the place of happiness.

ALEXANDER PUSHKIN (1799–1847) in *Eugene Onegin* (1833);
author of *The Captain's Daughter* (1836) and *The
Queen of Spades* (1834)

THE MORE YOU celebrate life, the more life there is to celebrate.

OPRAH WINFREY
chief creative officer, OWN television

I WOULD RATHER flirt with failure than never dance with my joy.

WES MOORE on *Super Soul Sunday*;
author of *The Work* (2014) and *The Other Wes Moore:
One Name, Two Fates* (2010); Rhodes Scholar

THE WILLINGNESS TO sacrifice is a necessary dimension of loving practice and living in community.

BELL HOOKS/Gloria Watkins (1952–2021) in *All
About Love: New Visions* (2000);
author; professor; feminist theorist; founder,
bell hooks Institute

CRUCIAL TO US thriving is creating the broadest table, with seats reserved for *all* of our people throughout the diaspora.

BRYANT TERRY in *Black Food* (2021);
chef-in-residence, Museum of the African Diaspora;
author of *Vegetable Kingdom* (2020) and *Afro-Vegan* (2014);
editor and curator of *Black Food*; food justice advocate

AS BLACK PEOPLE . . . we've got to be allowed to express all our feelings. There's something special about Black joy and Black hope, and there's something special about Black love.

COMMON/Lonnie Rashid Lynn Jr. in *Ebony*, July 2016;
rapper, actor, social justice advocate, author of *One Day It'll All Make Sense* (2011)

NOTHING TORTURES ME more than love. There is nothing in life that I experience more pain around than love. . . . The craving for love, for me, is far beyond the loss of death and far beyond the punishment of time.

WILL SMITH in a Holmes Place interview, 2016;
rapper, producer, winner of Academy Award for Best Actor (2022)

PEOPLE MAY NOT remember what you said, or what you did, but they will always remember how you make them *feel*!

> **MAYA ANGELOU** (1928–2014)
> poet, performer, author, social justice advocate

AS AFRICAN AMERICANS we have yet to talk enough about how individuals actually change, the conversion of the soul that must occur before the role of love and care and intimacy can be meaningfully talked about.

> **CORNEL WEST** in *Breaking Bread* (1991);
> professor, Harvard University; author of *Democracy
> Matters* (2004); social justice advocate

I BELIEVE THAT unarmed truth and unconditional love will have the final word.

> **MARTIN LUTHER KING JR.** (1929–1968) accepting
> the Nobel Peace Prize, 1964

LOVE SUPERSEDES ALL armies.

> **DICK GREGORY** (1932–2017)
> comedian, author, social justice advocate

LOVE IS NOT a gift. It is a diploma. A diploma conferring certain privileges: the privilege of expressing love and the privilege of receiving it.

TONI MORRISON (1931–2019) in *Paradise* (1997);
author, professor, recipient of Presidential Medal of
Freedom (2012), winner of Nobel Prize in Literature
(1993) and Pulitzer Prize for Fiction (1988)

I LEAVE YOU love. Love builds. It is positive and helpful.

MARY MCLEOD BETHUNE (1875–1955) in "Last Will
and Testament" (1955);
founder, Bethune-Cookman College; advisor to
President Franklin Roosevelt;
founder, National Council of Negro Women (1935)

LOVE IS AN expression of power we can use to transform our world.

ERICKA HUGGINS in the mural *Women of the Black
Panther Party*;
poet; social justice advocate; leader, Black
Panther Party; director, Oakland Community
School (1973–81)

AMERICA
CONTENDING MULTITUDES

We come from everywhere, and we contain
multitudes. . . .
BARACK OBAMA

IN AUGUST OF 1619, a ship appeared . . . in the English colony of Virginia. It carried more than 20 enslaved Africans, who were sold to the colonists. No aspect of the country that would be formed here has been untouched by the years of slavery that followed. On the 400th anniversary of this fateful moment, it is finally time to tell our story truthfully.

NIKOLE HANNAH-JONES in *The 1619 Project*;
author of *The 1619 Project: A New Origin Story* (2021),
winner of Pulitzer Prize for Commentary (2020),
2017 MacArthur Fellow

VOYAGE THROUGH DEATH
to life upon these shores.

ROBERT HAYDEN (1913–1980) in "Middle Passage"
from his *Selected Poems* (1966);
professor, essayist, U.S. Poet Laureate (1976–78)

WHILE THERE'S LIFE, there's hope.

TERENCE/PUBLIUS TERENTIUS AFER (195–159 BCE)
Carthaginian playwright during the Roman Republic

THE ORAL HISTORIES of enslaved people fundamentally changed me. . . . I don't think this nation will ever truly know the amount of evil committed under slavery and how that trauma is with us today.

> ADRIAN MILLER in *Stanford* magazine, March 2021;
> executive director, Colorado Council of Churches;
> culinary historian; barbecue judge; lawyer; public
> policy advisor; author of *Black Smoke* (2021), *The President's Kitchen Cabinet* (2017), and *Soul Food* (2013)

AMERICAN SLAVERY WAS a human horror of staggering proportions. It lasted twenty times longer than the Nazi Holocaust, killed ten times as many people, and destroyed cultures on three continents. The profits it produced endowed great fortunes and enriched generations.

> JULIAN BOND (1940–2015) in a 1976 speech;
> co-founder, SNCC; co-founder, Southern Poverty
> Law Center; author; essayist; poet; national chair,
> NAACP (1998–2009)

YOU ALL KNOW how Black humor started? It started on slave ships. Cat was rowing and dude says, "What you laughin' about?" He said, "Yesterday I was a king."

> RICHARD PRYOR (1940–2005) in *Pryor Convictions:
> And Other Life Sentences* (1995);
> comedian, actor

THE UNITED STATES was established by and for property-owning (read: wealthy) white men. The same make up as the majority of U.S. politicians at every level. . . . There is a range of retribution toward those who are not a part of that demographic.

> **MARK P. FANCHER** in "Where Incarceration Isn't the Answer," *YES! The Better Ideas Issue*, Fall 2020; human rights attorney, writer

AMERICA IS A country that has perfected leaving people behind. Over the course of our lifetime, America has really doubled and tripled down on the fact that the people with the most should have more, and the people with the least should have less.

> **W. KAMAU BELL** on the *Higher Learning* podcast, May 2021; comedian; author; filmmaker; host, Emmy Award–winning *United Shades of America*

HOW UNJUST IT is, that they who have but little should be always adding something to the wealth of the rich!

> **TERENCE/PUBLIUS TERENTIUS AFER** (195–159 BCE) Carthaginian playwright during the Roman Republic

PEOPLE ARE ALWAYS focusing on what do [looters] gain? . . . As long as we are focusing on *what* they're doing, we're not focusing on *why* they're doing it.

> **KIMBERLY JONES** in "How Can We Win?" speech, 2020;
> author of *How We Can Win* (2022) and *I'm Not Dying
> with You Tonight* (2019)

WHAT IS THE identity of America without Black people on their knees?

> **JANAYA FUTURE KHAN** on *Soul of a Nation*;
> storyteller; organizer; movement strategist;
> co-founder, Black Lives Matter, Toronto

[AMERICA WAS] FOUNDED on *ideals* of freedom, but the *practice* of slavery.

> **NIKOLE HANNAH-JONES** on *PBS NewsHour*;
> author of *The 1619 Project: A New Origin Story* (2021),
> winner of Pulitzer Prize for Commentary (2020),
> 2017 MacArthur Fellow

THE CONSTITUTION THEY devised was defective from the start, requiring several amendments, a civil war and momentous social transformation to attain the system of respect for individual freedoms and human rights we hold as fundamental today.

> THURGOOD MARSHALL (1908–1993) in *Black Enterprise*, August 1991; U.S. Supreme Court justice (1967–91)

I FELT SOMEHOW for many years that George Washington and Alexander Hamilton just left me out by mistake. But through the process of amendment, interpretation and court decision, I have finally been included in "We, the people."

> BARBARA JORDAN (1936–1996) in her opening statement at the Nixon impeachment hearings, 1974; U.S. representative (1973–79)

REMARKABLY, THE CONSTITUTION'S slow, steady change has regularly been in the direction of moral improvement. . . . [N]one but the living can own the Constitution. Those who wrote the version ratified centuries ago do not own the version we live by today. We do . . . and that fact is empowering.

> **DANIELLE ALLEN** in "The Flawed Genius of the
> Constitution," *The Atlantic*, October 2020;
> director, Center for Ethics, Harvard University; 2001
> MacArthur Fellow

H.R. 40 WAS an opportunity to have a commission to study reparations, but also a further context in which we look at slavery and the impact that it had on us.

> **DANNY GLOVER** on *Soul of the Nation*;
> actor, director, producer, social justice advocate

THE QUESTION OF civil rights is not the problem of [Black] people—it is the problem of the United States of America. . . . [America] cannot be a first-class power if it has second-class citizens.

> **ADAM CLAYTON POWELL JR.** (1908–1972) in a
> speech at Indiana University, 1964;
> U.S. representative (1945–71); pastor, Abyssinian
> Baptist Church; author

I AM NOT going ten thousand miles from here to help murder and kill and burn poor people simply to help continue the domination of white slave masters over the darker people. . . . If I'm going to die, I'll die right here fighting you! You my enemy. My enemy is white people. . . . You my opposer when I want freedom. You my opposer when I want justice. You my opposer when I want equality.

MUHAMMAD ALI (1942–2016) refusing U.S. Army
induction, 1967;
three-time heavyweight boxing champion, philanthropist, social justice hero, author of *The Soul of a
Butterfly* (2003) and *The Greatest* (1975)

WE CAN HATE niggas, but y'all can't. And the reason y'all can't is because y'all don't deal with enough [niggas and Black folks] to know how to distinguish between the two.

CHARLAMAGNE THA GOD/Lenard McKelvey on
"Chris Rock's *Bring the Pain*," *Cultureshock*, 2018;
co-host, *The Breakfast Club*; author of *Black Privilege*
(2017) and *Shook One* (2018)

To say that the attack on the U.S. Capitol . . . is not part of our history . . . is a bald-faced denial. But the denial is normal. In the aftermath of catastrophes, when have Americans commonly admitted who we are? The heartbeat of America is denial.

> **IBRAM X. KENDI** in "Denial Is the Heartbeat of
> America," *The Atlantic*, January 2021;
> director, Boston University Center for Antiracist
> Research; author of *How to Raise an Antiracist* (2022)
> and *How to Be an Antiracist* (2019); *Time* 100 Most
> Influential (2020)

The American idea is indeed in trouble. It should be. We have told ourselves a story that secures our virtues and protects us from our vices. But today we confront the ugliness of who we are—our darker angels reign.

> **EDDIE S. GLAUDE JR.** in *Begin Again* (2020);
> distinguished professor of African American studies,
> Princeton University

This country needs healing. Healing cannot happen without admission. It can't happen without the full recognition of the truth. The country was BUILT on systemic racism and oppression. The foundation is rotten.

> **ANGELA RYE** in an April 26, 2021, tweet;
> CEO, Impact Strategies; political analyst, CNN and NPR

IF YOU HAVE any interest in seeing things get better, you might want to know history.

> WHOOPI GOLDBERG/Caryn Elaine Johnson on *The View*, February 2021; actor, comedian, author, EGOT winner

ONE OF THE most perverted political sayings is someone saying they are colorblind. I don't want you to be color-blind, I want you to see the value that I bring, the richness of the culture that I represent. There's a fear of replacement by some and a cultural anxiety from others, and that becomes combustible.

> BAKARI SELLERS in *Colorlines*, May 2021; CNN commentator, lawyer, author of *My Vanishing Country* (2020)

WE COME FROM everywhere, and we contain multitudes. And that has always been both the promise of America, and also what makes America sometimes so contentious.

> BARACK OBAMA in the *New York Times*, December 2020; president of the United States (2009–17); author of *A Promised Land* (2020)

ONE OF THE most singular facts about the unwritten history of this country is the consummate ability with which Southern influence, Southern ideas, Southern ideals, have from the very beginning even up to the present day, dictated to and domineered over the brain and sinew of this nation.

> ANNA JULIA COOPER (1858–1964) in *A Voice from the South* (1892); educator, social justice advocate

REAL TRAGEDY IS never resolved. It goes on hopelessly forever.

> CHINUA ACHEBE (1930–2013) in *No Longer at Ease* (1960); author of *Things Fall Apart* (1958), professor

SLAVERY WAS JUST one small part of a loan that Black people invested into America. . . . The fantasy that we call the "American Dream" isn't solely funded by decency, hard work, or American exceptionalism. It comes from theft.

> MICHAEL HARRIOT in *YES! The Black Lives Issue*, Fall 2020; senior writer, *The Root*; author of *Black AF History* (2021)

POLICING [IN THE South] starts with slave catchers. These are men who go around at night to make sure that enslaved people are not leaving their plantations. But they are also there to terrorize, to intimidate.

GRETCHEN SORIN on the PBS documentary *Driving While Black: Race, Space and Mobility in America* (2020); director, Cooperstown Graduate Program; author of *Driving While Black* (2020)

OUR POLICING SYSTEM is built to enable white supremacy. It is not just a few bad apples, it's a rotten tree. We need to transform public safety—and that starts with defunding the police and reinvesting in our communities.

CORI BUSH in a February 17, 2021, tweet; U.S. representative (2021–)

OUR LIVES ARE being shot and choked out of us, and our broken bodies left behind are spectacles on social media and news outlets. Our cruel deaths always come with a remarkable show of mental gymnastics from white America as they grasp for any reason to explain why we deserve to die.

ANNIKA LONDON in "My Grandmother's Search for Security," *Inkstick*, 2021; senior digital associate, Win Without War Education Fund

KILLERS AND DANGEROUS drug dealers go to prison when they get caught. Dangerous cops often aren't even charged for their bad acts. That makes them more powerful, and scarier.

ISSAC BAILEY in "Why Should a Cop's Blue Fear Matter More Than My Black Life?" on CNN.com; journalist; professor, Davidson College

WHY ARE POLICE the only ones who are entitled to fear? The people who are armed & trained to run into dangerous situations are entitled to act out of fear, but not the civilian who is approached by a cop knowing that cops assault & kill people for no reason?

BREE NEWSOME BASS in an April 15, 2021, tweet; artist, social justice advocate, Confederate flag remover

[THE MASSACRE OF school children in Uvalde is] another reminder that we can't just trust what the police say. . . . Journalists shouldn't be reporting what the police said, they should be investigating what actually happened.

TREVOR NOAH on *The Daily Show with Trevor Noah*, June 2022; comedian, writer, producer

THE EXTRACTION OF Black people's labor, the use of Black people's bodies; their capacity to produce and generate wealth required, in fact, restrictions on their ability to move. . . . And so much of American history, so much of American law is actually focused on policing that mobility.

CRAIG STEVEN WILDER on the PBS documentary *Driving While Black: Race, Space and Mobility in America* (2020); professor of American history, MIT; author of *Ebony & Ivy* (2013)

UNTIL THE KILLING of Black mothers' sons becomes as important to the rest of the country as the killing of white mothers' sons, we who believe in freedom cannot rest.

ELLA BAKER (1903–1986) director of branches, NAACP; organizer, SCLC and SNCC

FOR AS LONG as whites enforce equality in the price of railroad tickets, and in every other particular, where we are required to pay and do, and be punished, some of us will believe that equality should be carried to a finish.

HENRY MCNEAL TURNER (1834–1915) bishop, African Methodist Episcopal Church; elected to Georgia legislature in 1868, but not allowed to serve

IN THE SOUTH they don't care how close you get so long as you don't get too high. In the North they don't care how high you get so long as you don't get too close.

AFRICAN AMERICAN FOLK SAYING

HOUSING ACCOMPLISHED IN the North everything that Jim Crow accomplished in the South.

NIKOLE HANNAH-JONES on *Black America Since MLK: And Still I Rise* (2016); author of *The 1619 Project: A New Origin Story* (2021), winner of Pulitzer Prize for Commentary (2020), 2017 MacArthur Fellow

SLAVERY IN THIS land . . . was an American innovation, an American institution created by and for the benefit of the elites of the dominant caste and enforced by poorer members of the dominant caste who tied their lot to the caste system rather than to their consciences.

ISABEL WILKERSON in *Caste: The Origins of Our Discontents* (2020); author of *The Warmth of Other Suns* (2010), winner of Pulitzer Prize for Feature Writing (1994)

To PLUNDER A people of everything, you must plunder their humanity first. . . . There is an insidious cost to this—a man invents a monster to justify his brutality, only to find the monster is within.

> TA-NEHISI COATES in "The Pyromancer's Dream,"
> *Vanity Fair*, 2020;
> author of *The Water Dancer* (2019) and *Between the World and Me* (2015), 2015 MacArthur Fellow

THIS IS HOW Black people get killed, when you send them home and they don't know how to fight for themselves. I had to talk to somebody, maybe the media, somebody, to let people know how I'm being treated up in this place.

> SUSAN MOORE in a December 2020 Facebook post
> from her hospital bed;
> Indiana physician who died from COVID-19 after
> delayed treatment

THIS IS A system that most people would have you believe is broke. The system is not broke! The system won exactly the way it was designed to win.

> ANTHONY RAY HINTON on *Soul of a Nation*;
> twenty-eight years on death row in Alabama before
> exoneration with no compensation, author of *The
> Sun Does Shine* (2018)

WE ARE CAUGHT in a system that needs to be dismantled. . . . [the film *When They See Us*] in addition to being
compelling . . . is also teaching folks how to act around
police and what not to do.

> **AVA DUVERNAY** on a *Breakfast Club* interview, May 2019;
> award-winning filmmaker, writer, producer, director

[STILL EMPLOYED] TULSA police officer . . . shot
and killed my twin brother, Terence Crutcher. . . . The
state-sanctioned violence against Black people by racist
police officers is directly tied to the legacy of slavery in
this country.

> **TIFFANY CRUTCHER** in a Color of Change repara-
> tions petition, October 2020

THE DEATH PENALTY in this country isn't a topic that
can be resolved by asking whether people deserve to die
for the crimes they've committed. I think the threshold
question is, "Do we deserve to kill?" . . . The death penalty
is the stepchild of lynching.

> **BRYAN STEVENSON** on *Soul of a Nation*;
> founder and executive director, Equal Justice Initiative;
> 2016 MacArthur Fellow; author of *Just Mercy* (2014)

I HAVE ALWAYS been against the death penalty. . . . I believe it is a relic of barbarism and savagery and that it is inconsistent with decent morals and the teachings of Christian ethics.

KWAME NKRUMAH (1909–1972)
first prime minister of independent Ghana,
author, revolutionary

AT BOTTOM, WHAT makes a community safe is not the number of guns, but the number of good schools, the number of good jobs, . . . of educational opportunities . . . of opportunities people have for living a decent life.

MICHELLE ALEXANDER in a University of Chicago
lecture, 2013;
author of *The New Jim Crow* (2010), lawyer,
professor, social justice advocate

IF YOU ARE not coming to the people's defense, then don't challenge us. . . . Don't talk to us about looting! Ya'll are the looters; looting Black people. America looted Native Americans when [Europeans] first came here. Looting is what you do. We learned it from you. We learned violence from you. . . . So, if you want us to do better; *you* do better!

TAMIKA D. MALLORY in a Minneapolis speech, June 2020;
author of *State of Emergency: How We Win in the
Country We Built* (2021); co-chair, Women's March on
Washington (2017)

THE REAL CRIMINALS in this society are not all of the people who populate the prisons across the state, but those who have stolen the wealth of the world from the people.

ANGELA Y. DAVIS
professor emerita, University of California, Santa Cruz; social justice advocate; author of *Freedom Is a Constant Struggle* (2015)

HERE, EQUAL JUSTICE under the law is prescribed only for the corporate rich and powerful. There are literally thousands of people imprisoned solely because of their race and poverty.

BENJAMIN F. CHAVIS JR.
national director, Million Man March (1995); co-founder, Hip-Hop Summit Action Network

MASS INCARCERATION HAS fundamentally changed our world. . . . We have a system of justice in this country that treats you much better if you're rich and guilty than if you're poor and innocent. Wealth, not culpability, shapes outcomes.

BRYAN STEVENSON in a March 2012 TED Talk; founder and executive director, Equal Justice Initiative; 2016 MacArthur Fellow; author of *Just Mercy* (2014)

[PRISON] REINFORCES EVERYTHING you've been taught negative about yourself. And that becomes the more negative you are, the more validated you are in that environment.

SHAKA SENGHOR on *Super Soul Sunday*;
author of *Writing My Wrongs: Life, Death, and Redemption in an American Prison* (2016), entrepreneur, speaker, consultant

[PRISON] ABOLITION SEEKS to undo the way of thinking and doing things that sees prison and punishment as solutions for all kinds of social, economic, political, behavioral and interpersonal problems. Abolition, though, is not simply decarceration, put everybody out on the street. It is reorganizing how we live our lives together in the world.

RUTH WILSON GILMORE in "The Case for Prison Abolition," *Democracy Now!*, May 2020; professor of earth and environmental sciences, City University of New York; prison abolitionist

CAPITALISM IS ROOTED in a civilization that is based on *difference*. This doesn't at all mean that white people are the enemy, or that Black people are all victims. . . . It doesn't mean that all white people benefit. It just simply means that capitalism is structured through *difference*.

ROBIN D. G. KELLEY in the *Los Angeles Times*, 2021; professor of American history, UCLA; author of *Thelonious Monk* (2009), *Freedom Dreams* (2002), and *Race Rebels* (1994)

MONOPOLY CAPITALISM IS bigger than government—it buys and sells governments.

> **HARRY BELAFONTE** in "Belafonte's Balancing Act,"
> the *New Yorker*, 1996;
> singer, actor, social justice advocate, author of
> *My Song* (2011)

THE APPEARANCE OF millionaires in any society is no proof of its affluence; they can be produced by very poor countries. . . . It is not efficiency of production which makes millionaires; it is the uneven distribution of what is produced.

> **JULIUS KAMBARAGE NYERERE** (1922–1999)
> first president of independent Tanzania (1964–85);
> author of "Ujamaa—The Basis for African Socialism";
> co-founder, Organization of African Unity

SOMEHOW WE ARE going to have to develop a concept of *enough* for those at the top and at the bottom so that the necessities of the many are not sacrificed for the luxuries of the few.

> **MARIAN WRIGHT EDELMAN**
> founder and president emerita, Children's Defense
> Fund; author of *The State of America's Children* (2000)
> and *Families in Peril* (1987)

THE CHALLENGE WE have to address is how do we make an economy in this globalized, technological environment that's working for everybody?

> **BARACK OBAMA** on *My Next Guest Needs No Introduction with David Letterman*;
> president of the United States (2009–17), author of
> *A Promised Land* (2020)

WE MUST DEFUND law enforcement and reimagine a world that relies on an economy of care versus an economy of punishment.

> **PATRISSE KHAN-CULLORS** on Instagram;
> *Time* 100 Most Influential (2020); author of *When They Call You a Terrorist* (2018); co-founder, Black Lives Matter (2013)

I DON'T WANT people to ever forget who Sandra Bland is. We can't keep filing these [police murders] away and forgetting about them without drawing some kind of conclusions about why they happen.

> **MALCOLM GLADWELL** on *Super Soul Sunday*;
> journalist, author of *Talking to Strangers* (2019) and
> *The Tipping Point* (2000)

WE CREATE CATEGORIES to make sense of the world, to assert some control and coherence to the stimuli that we're constantly being bombarded with. . . . Yet, just as the categories we create allow us to make quick decisions, they also reinforce bias. So the very things that help us to see the world also can blind us to it. They render our choices effortless, friction-free. Yet they exact a heavy toll.

> **JENNIFER EBERHARDT** in a 2020 TED Talk;
> author of *Biased: Uncovering the Hidden Prejudice
> That Shapes What We See, Think, and Do* (2019); 2014
> MacArthur Fellow; professor of psychology,
> Stanford University

THE PRACTICE OF assessing human beings by their standard deviation from whiteness has run its course in the Americas. Labels are not bad, per se, if they remain one-dimensional descriptors, but they never do, do they? They morph into three-dimensional containers for prejudice.

> **CELESTE MOHAMMED** in *The Common*, January 2021;
> author of *Pleasantview: A Novel in Stories* (2021)

WE HAVE WITNESSED two systems of justice: one that let extremists storm the U.S. Capitol yesterday, and another that released tear gas on peaceful protestors last summer. It's simply unacceptable.

> **KAMALA HARRIS** in a January 7, 2021, tweet;
> vice president of the United States (2021–)

THE CRIME IS not what we *do*; it's who we *are*!

MICHAEL ERIC DYSON on *Real Time with Bill Maher*,
November 2020;
sociologist, professor, author of *Long Time Coming* (2020)

THE U.S. WILL never achieve true national security so long as it believes that the lives of people of color, here and abroad, must be destroyed in order to accomplish this goal.

ANNIKA LONDON in "My Grandmother's Search for Security," *Inkstick*, 2021;
senior digital associate, Win Without War Education Fund

WE KNOW THAT had the insurrectionists been Black or Brown they would also be dead. In America, we reserve the right of revolution for those who've always had the most power. Sometimes they revolt in the form of mob violence. Other times it's the quiet theft of trillions from the treasury or the suppression of votes through legal bribery and gerrymandering. The result is the same.

BARATUNDE THURSTON in "Recommentunde,"
January 6, 2021;
author of *How to Be Black* (2012), comedian, cultural critic

THESE DAYS WE'RE experiencing a flood—not of facts but factoids, not of truth but truthiness. . . . Untruths spread faster and faster, at the click of a mouse, spawning whole faux movements like birthers and truthers, billionaire populists and the alt-right, whose euphemistic names describe exactly what they do **not** believe.

KEVIN YOUNG in *Bunk: The Rise of Hoaxes, Humbug,
Plagiarists, Phonies, Post-Facts, and Fake News* (2017);
award-winning poet and author; poetry editor, the
New Yorker; director, National Museum of African
American History and Culture

THERE IS A term, "accountability and consequences." You hear it used all the time in the criminal justice system, and almost always it is directed at the person who is arrested, never at the system itself and the people who work in the system. But . . . there must be consequences when someone breaks the law and that includes police officers.

KAMALA HARRIS on *The Daily Social Distancing Show
with Trevor Noah*, October 2020;
vice president of the United States (2021–)

WE CAN BREATHE a little easier [since the presidential inauguration], but that's no reason to retreat to the sidelines. All of us must remain engaged in the work of justice. Change doesn't come *from* Washington, it comes *to* Washington.

CORY BOOKER in a January 2021 tweet;
lawyer, author, U.S. senator (2013–)

EVERY BIT OF social change has been made from the bottom up. So laws change because people's voices are heard.

BARACK OBAMA on ESPN film *37 Words* (2022);
president of the United States (2009–17), author of
A Promised Land (2020)

THE USA SPENDS roughly $180 billion a year on policing and prisons. Homelessness in America could be ended by spending 1/10th of that amount. This isn't about public safety or smart economic spending. It's about racism and violent state oppression.

BREE NEWSOME BASS in a December 3, 2020, tweet;
artist, social justice advocate, Confederate flag remover

YOU CANNOT DIVORCE Confederate iconography from the treatment of African Americans as second-class citizens of this country during Jim Crow and now.

> **JULIAN HAYTER** in the *New York Times*, June 2020;
> social justice advocate; historian, University of Richmond

WHAT BECAME CLEAR was that, for [the Sons of Confederate Veterans], history isn't the story of what actually happened, it is just the story they want to believe.

> **CLINT SMITH** in "Inheritance," *The Atlantic* project
> to explore the ignored legacy and experiences of
> Black Americans, June 2021;
> author of *How the Word Is Passed* (2021) and
> *Counting Descent* (2016)

A GOVERNMENT WHICH uses force to maintain its rule teaches the oppressed to use force to oppose it.

> **ROLIHLAHLA NELSON MANDELA** (1918–2013)
> incarcerated for resisting apartheid (1963–90),
> president of South Africa (1994–99)

THERE ARE NO good times to be Black in America, but some times are worse than others.

> **DAVID BRADLEY** in *Esquire*, May 1982;
> author of *The Chaneysville Incident* (1981) and *South Street*
> (1975); professor of creative writing, University of Oregon

A PANDEMIC DOES not erase inequality; it exacerbates it.

> **BRITTANY PACKNETT CUNNINGHAM** on *Black Women OWN the Conversation*; contributor for NBC News and MSNBC; fellow, Institute of Politics, Harvard University; author; social justice advocate

TRUTH-TELLERS ARE NOT always palatable. There is a preference for candy bars.

> **GWENDOLYN BROOKS** (1917–2000) in *Winnie* (1988); winner of Pulitzer Prize for Poetry (1950); Illinois Poet Laureate

TRUTH IS THAT which serves the interests of a people. Two groups of people locked in combat cannot be expected to have the same truth.

> **ALBERT B. CLEAGE JR.** (1911–2000) in *Black Christian Nationalism* (1972); founder, Shrine of the Black Madonna Church and Shrine Cultural Center and Bookstore

RACISM IS IN large measure a form of psychological warfare.

> **JOHNNETTA COLE** in *Conversations* (1993); anthropologist; president, Bennett College (2002–07) and Spelman College (1987–97); author of *Gender Talk: The Struggle for Women's Equality in African American Communities* (2003)

IT IS A contradiction to protect minority rights in the [U.S.] Senate while refusing to protect minority rights in the society. . . . Are we going to stand on the side of truth and righteousness and justice? . . . This is a defining moment in the American nation and all of us have a role to play.

RAPHAEL WARNOCK on CNN, March 2021;
pastor, Ebenezer Baptist Church; U.S. senator (2021–)

IN A RACIALLY divided society, majority rule may become majority tyranny.

LANI GUINIER (1950–2022) in *The Tyranny of the Majority* (1994);
author; professor, Harvard Law School

COLOR IS NOT a human or a personal reality; it is a political reality.

JAMES BALDWIN (1924–1987) in *The Fire Next Time* (1963);
essayist, novelist, playwright, social justice advocate

AFRICAN AMERICAN CRIME to many white race-relations experts stood as an almost singular reflection of Black culture and humanity.

KHALIL GIBRAN MUHAMMAD in *The Condemnation of Blackness* (2010);
professor of history, race, and public policy, Harvard University

OUR AMERICA IS frightened of fact, of history, of processes, of necessity. It hugs the easy way of damning those whom it cannot understand, of excluding those who look different, and it salves its conscience with a self-draped cloak of righteousness.

RICHARD WRIGHT (1908–1960) in *American Hunger* (1944);
author of *White Man, Listen!* (1957), *Black Boy* (1945),
and *Native Son* (1940); social justice advocate

THE COLD WAR did a lot to advance civil rights because the United States could not afford to appear as a repressive, segregated, violent nation that didn't respect the rights of Black people.

ALLYSON HOBBS in *Stanford* magazine, September 2020;
professor of history; director, African and African
American Studies program, Stanford University

THERE WILL BE a cost—and not just a moral one—if Georgia continues its march backward. [If] there is an impediment to the leadership's plunging the state back into its ugly past, it will likely not be for love of democracy or the Constitution. It will be for reverence of another piece of paper that embodies deeply held American values: the dollar bill.

JELANI COBB in the *New Yorker*, March 2021;
dean, Columbia University journalism school; staff
writer, the *New Yorker*; author of *The Substance of Hope:
Barack Obama and the Paradox of Progress* (2010)

THE AMAZING THING about this country is that the past matters only in the ways we want the past to matter. We can't say the Declaration of Independence still matters, or the Constitution still matters, but 1619 doesn't, but slavery doesn't, but Jim Crow doesn't. . . . We can't be liberated from this legacy [of racism] if we don't acknowledge the role that legacy plays right now.

NIKOLE HANNAH-JONES on *United Shades of America
with W. Kamau Bell*, 2020;
author of *The 1619 Project: A New Origin Story* (2021),
winner of Pulitzer Prize for Commentary (2020),
2017 MacArthur Fellow

I EXPECTED TO go to these plantations where I'd be told the history of my ancestors, and what I got instead was a proliferation of tourist attractions meant for the white gaze. . . . In a place that Black people built, lived, and died, often violent deaths, they were not even the story.

LATANYA MCQUEEN in "What Visiting Plantations
Taught Me About Historical Erasure," *Literary Hub*,
August 2021;
author of *When the Reckoning Comes* (2021);
professor of English, Coe College

FOR DECADES, POLITICIANS stoked and exploited white resentment. Corporations consolidated their hold on government and cut American workers off at the knees. Ideas of the public good were reduced to an unrelenting pursuit of self-interest. . . . A moral reckoning is upon us, and we have to decide, once and for all, whether or not we will truly be a multiracial democracy.

EDDIE S. GLAUDE JR. in *Begin Again* (2020);
distinguished professor of African American studies,
Princeton University

THE COUNTRY'S DEMOGRAPHIC revolution over the past fifty years has given birth to a New American Majority. Progressive people of color now comprise 23 percent of all the eligible voters in America, and progressive Whites account for 28 percent of all eligible voters.

STEVE PHILLIPS in *Brown Is the New White* (2016);
civil rights lawyer; senior fellow, Center for
American Progress

FEW PROBLEMS HAVE ever been solved by ignoring them. . . . Whatever is lurking will fester whether you choose to look or not. Ignorance is no protection from the consequences of inaction.

ISABEL WILKERSON in *Caste: The Origins of Our
Discontents* (2020);
author of *The Warmth of Other Suns* (2010), winner of
Pulitzer Prize for Feature Writing (1994)

YOU HAVE TO assess every situation that you're in and you have to decide, is this happening because I'm Black? Is this happening because I'm a woman? Or is this happening because this is how it happens?

CHARLAYNE HUNTER-GAULT
former news correspondent for CNN, PBS, and NPR;
social justice advocate

MY [REPUBLICAN] PARTY may have given up its voice
on things that matter but I have not. This [2020 national]
election is about the course of a nation and the character
of her people reflected in the leader they choose. America
matters.

MICHAEL STEELE in an October 20, 2020, tweet;
lieutenant governor of Maryland (2003–07); former
chair, Republican National Committee

I CANNOT ACCEPT the definition of collective good as
articulated by a privileged minority in society, especially
when that minority is in power.

WOLE SOYINKA
playwright, poet, essayist, winner of Nobel Prize in
Literature (1986)

WHITE FOLKS DON'T understand about the blues. They
hear it come out, but they don't know how it got there. . . .
You don't sing to feel better. You sing 'cause that's a way
of understanding life.

AUGUST WILSON (1945–2005) in *Ma Rainey's Black
Bottom* (1981);
Tony Award– and Pulitzer Prize–winning playwright

THE BLUES HAS been the foundation for all other American music since the beginning.

> WILLIE DIXON (1915–1992) in *I Am the Blues* (1989);
> blues musician, vocalist, songwriter, arranger,
> record producer

IN OUR CULTURE whiteness is rarely marked . . . and the majoritarian privilege of never noticing themselves was the beginning of an imbalance from which so much else flowed.

> PATRICIA J. WILLIAMS in *Seeing a Color-Blind
> Future* (1997);
> legal scholar, columnist, 2000 MacArthur Fellow

SOME WHITE PEOPLE are so accustomed to operating at a competitive advantage that when the playing field is level, they feel handicapped.

> NATHAN MCCALL in *Makes Me Wanna Holler* (1994);
> journalist, author

SLAVERY WAS . . . AN unnecessarily cruel and repressive method of making money for the Western white man. Colonialism was a more subtle, but equally repressive method of accomplishing the same end.

> AMIRI BARAKA/LEROI JONES (1934–2014) in *Home:
> Social Essays* (1966);
> playwright, poet, essayist

THOSE FORCES WHICH stand against the freedom of nations are not only wrong—they are doomed to utter defeat and dishonor. . . . Colored peoples of the world are going to be free and equal no matter whose "best interests" are in the way.

PAUL ROBESON (1898–1976)
singer, actor, social justice advocate

INJUSTICE ANYWHERE IS a threat to justice everywhere.

MARTIN LUTHER KING JR. (1929–1968) in "Letter
from a Birmingham Jail," 1963;
Nobel Peace Prize winner (1964)

DEMOCRACY, LIKE RELIGION, never was designed to make . . . profits less.

ZORA NEALE HURSTON (1891–1960) in *Dust Tracks
on a Road* (1942);
folklorist, anthropologist, author of *Their Eyes Were
Watching God* (1937)

THE WEST IS dying of the effects of its compulsive hatred, and its obsessive wish for revenge.

ALLISON DAVIS (1902–1983) in *Leadership, Love, and
Aggression* (1983);
anthropologist, professor, author

AMERICANS TOO OFTEN resolve their trivial arguments by shooting one another to death. . . . We make a mistake if we try to separate gang and drug violence from the overall violent context of American life.

DEBORAH PROTHROW-STITH in *Deadly Consequences* (1991); dean and professor of medicine, Charles R. Drew University College of Medicine; co-author of *Sugar and Spice and No Longer Nice* (2005)

GIVEN THE CHOICE, [America has] decided to get rid of children rather than guns. We've absurdly interpreted the Constitution to defend this madness while forgetting that the Constitution can be changed while dead children cannot be brought back to life.

BARATUNDE THURSTON in "America, In Memoriam," *Recommentunde*, May 30, 2022; author of *How to Be Black* (2012), comedian, cultural critic

BEING PRESIDENT [OF the United States] doesn't change who you are; it *reveals* who you are.

MICHELLE OBAMA at the 2012 Democratic National Convention; First Lady of the United States (2009–17); author of *Becoming* (2018)

DATA [FOR BLACKS] is most often used to tell a story of continuing inequities. . . . [T]he danger of such an emphasis is that it too often only serves to reinforce a collective sense of inferiority by suggesting that Blacks never quite measure up.

AUDREY EDWARDS and CRAIG K. POLITE in *Children of the Dream: The Psychology of Black Success* (1992); award-winning journalist, author (Edwards); clinical psychologist (Polite)

WE'RE ALWAYS TALKING about Blacks as a group and whites as individuals.

JOHN HOPE FRANKLIN (1915–2009)
historian, author of *Mirror to America* (2005) and *From Slavery to Freedom* (1947)

[RACE] LOCKS WHITE people in a morally and ethically indefensible position they must preserve by force. . . . The pervasive violence in our society . . . is rooted in the paradigm of race.

JOHN EDGAR WIDEMAN in *Fatheralong* (1994); professor, essayist, award-winning novelist

DOMINANT RELIGION IS always explicitly violent against people who have no power. . . . That's true anywhere in the world. . . . The crucifixion was a first century lynching. . . . America has a tradition of lynching Black people. . . . When you see a lynched Black body, that's who God is. God is present in that body.

JAMES H. CONE (1938–2018) in a Trinity Church
interview, 2010;
founder, Black liberation theology; author of *The Cross
and the Lynching Tree* (2011), *A Black Theology of Liberation* (1970), and *Black Theology & Black Power* (1969)

RAGE DOESN'T NEED reason. It only needs targets.

CLARENCE PAGE
syndicated columnist for the *Chicago Tribune*; winner
of Pulitzer Prize for Commentary (1989)

VIOLENCE HAS NO redemption in it.

JESSE JACKSON on the PBS documentary *Black
America Since MLK: And Still I Rise* (2016);
candidate for U.S. president (1984, 1988); founder,
Rainbow/PUSH Coalition; author of *Keeping Hope
Alive* (2019) and *Legal Lynching* (1996)

ONLY WHITE PEOPLE have been legitimized as makers of American history. Black people have become history's instruments.

CHUCK STONE (1924–2014) in *Black Political Power in America* (1968); journalist, author

UP CLOSE, MOST white folks, like most people, are mediocre. They've just rigged the system to privilege themselves and disadvantage everyone else.

JILL NELSON in *Volunteer Slavery* (1993); journalist, author of *Let's Get It On* (2007) and *Straight, No Chaser* (1997)

WHITE FOLKS LOVE to use that word to describe us. *Articulate.* It means we don't grunt like jungle savages.

PAUL MOONEY (1941–2021) in *Black Is the New White* (2009); comedian, writer, actor

THERE IS NOTHING more dangerous than to build a society with a large segment of people in it who feel they have no stake in it; who feel they have nothing to lose.

MARTIN LUTHER KING JR. (1929–1968) Nobel Peace Prize winner (1964)

RACISM SYSTEMATICALLY VERIFIES itself anytime the slave can only be free by imitating his master.

JAMIL ABDULLAH AL-AMIN/H. RAP BROWN
chair, SNCC (1967–71); author of *Revolution by the Book* (1993) and *Die Nigger Die!* (1969)

WE DON'T HATE nobody because of their color. We hate *oppression*!

BOBBY SEALE
author of *Seize the Time* (1970); co-founder, Black Panther Party (1966)

THE UNITED STATES . . . becomes the world's most interesting laboratory for working out the intricate issues of race adjustment.

KELLY MILLER (1863–1939) in *Race Adjustment* (1908); professor of mathematics and sociology, Howard University; author of *Out of the House of Bondage* (1914)

[I BELIEVED] THAT the story of my family, and my efforts to understand that story, might speak in some way to the fissures of race that have characterized the American experience.

BARACK OBAMA in *Dreams from My Father* (2004); president of the United States (2009–17); author of *A Promised Land* (2020)

SEEING OUR WORLD through the lens of community is so important. . . . [L]et's challenge ourselves to build communities of compassion.

MEGHAN MARKLE on *TIME100*, 2020;
actor, Duchess of Sussex

THEY'VE BEEN ENACTING violence against our bodies since the first one was kidnapped and brought here hundreds of years ago. And we're still standing, right? We're still here and we're still fighting. And you can look at most marginalized communities that are under attack by white supremacy and say the same thing right in our own beautiful, very human ways.

CAT BROOKS in a KQED interview, 2021;
executive director, Justice Teams Network; co-founder,
Anti Police-Terror Project; playwright; poet

WHILE TODAY'S TERRIBLE display of terror and meanness shakes us, let's remember: Jon Ossoff, Jewish son of an immigrant & Reverend Warnock, first Black Senator from Georgia, will join a Catholic POTUS & the first woman, Black + Indian VP in our nation's capital. God bless America.

STACEY ABRAMS in a January 6, 2021, tweet;
lawyer; entrepreneur; founder, Fair Fight; author of
Lead from the Outside (2018)

AMERICA NEVER WAS America to me,
And yet I swear this oath—
America will be!

LANGSTON HUGHES (1902–1967) in "Let America Be
America Again";
author, playwright, essayist, poet

NOT EVERYTHING IS lost. Responsibility cannot be lost,
it can only be abdicated. If one refuses abdication, one
begins again.

JAMES BALDWIN in *Just Above My Head* (1979);
essayist, novelist, playwright, social justice advocate

CHALLENGES
CREATING OPPORTUNITIES

I had to make my own living and my own
opportunity.
MADAM C. J. WALKER

IN EVERY CRISIS there is a message. Crises are nature's way of forcing change—breaking down old structures, shaking loose negative habits so something new and better can take their place.

SUSAN L. TAYLOR
editor-in-chief, *Essence* (1981–2000); author of
Lessons in Living (1995)

[THOSE] WHO START behind in the great race of life must forever remain behind or run faster than the [people] in front.

BENJAMIN E. MAYS (1894–1984)
author of *Born to Rebel* (1971); president, Morehouse
College (1940–67)

TO BE BLACK is to live with anger as the defining emotion of a racial experience. . . . What all achieving Blacks successfully do is turn the color of Black into the color of victory.

AUDREY EDWARDS and **CRAIG K. POLITE** in *Children of the Dream: The Psychology of Black Success* (1992); award-winning journalist, author (Edwards); clinical psychologist (Polite)

THERE'S NO SUCH thing as failure. It's just God trying to move you in a new direction.

OPRAH WINFREY
chief creative officer, OWN television

IT'S SO EASY when the money is flashed before you to allow that to govern your choices. I don't really work for money. I work because there are certain issues that I wish to address about myself as a Black woman and about my race.

CICELY TYSON (1924–2021)
actor, author of *Just As I Am* (2021), Television
Academy Hall of Fame honoree (2020), recipient of
Presidential Medal of Freedom (2016), Tony Award
winner (2014), Emmy Award winner (1994, 1974)

LET [RACISM] BE a problem to someone else. . . . Let it drag them down. Don't use it as an excuse for your own shortcomings.

COLIN POWELL (1937–2021)
U.S. secretary of state (2001–05), four-star general,
author of *It Worked for Me* (2012) and *My American
Journey* (1995)

A BITTER PERSON is a person in the process of [self-destruction].

DEMPSEY J. TRAVIS (1920–2009)
entrepreneur, author of *An Autobiography of Black
Chicago* (1981)

WHEN YOU CONTROL a [person's] thinking, you do not have to worry about [their] actions. You will not have to tell [them] not to stand here or go yonder. [They] will find [their] "proper place" and will stay in it.

CARTER G. WOODSON (1875–1950) in
The Mis-Education of the Negro (1933);
historian; author; founder, Negro History Week (1926)

IF WE MAKE decisions based on how white supremacists may view our behavior, then they control what we do. Our integrity should be more important than their gaze.

JANET CHEATHAM BELL
author of *The Time and Place That Gave Me Life*
(2007), curator of this collection

I DIDN'T WANT to make a choice like [leaving *The Chappelle Show*,] then be a parable of what not to do. The best part about quitting was coming back here [to Yellow Springs, Ohio]. I started realizing the value of community. . . . I'm very happy that I did what I did.

DAVE CHAPPELLE on *My Next Guest Needs No Introduction with David Letterman*; comedian, actor, winner of Mark Twain Prize for American Humor (2019)

WHEN LIFE KNOCKS you down try to fall on your back because if you can look up, you can get up.

LES BROWN
motivational speaker, author of *It's Not Over Until You Win* (1997) and *Live Your Dreams* (1992)

IT DOESN'T MATTER how many times you fall down. What matters is how many times you get up.

MARIAN WRIGHT EDELMAN in *The Measure of Our Success* (1992); founder and president emerita, Children's Defense Fund; author of *The State of America's Children* (2000) and *Families in Peril* (1987)

I HAD TO make my own living and my own opportunity. . . . Don't sit down and wait for the opportunities to come; you have to get up and make them.

MADAM C. J. WALKER (1867–1919)
entrepreneur, philanthropist, social justice advocate

THAT'S THE BEAUTIFUL thing about being a Black business owner now is knowing that there is precedent for what I'm building. But there's also an anxiety because if you took it out the first time [1921 Tulsa massacre] and you took it out again [urban renewal]; if I look towards the horizon, I'm worried about what is that next thing that's coming to destroy this again?

ONIKAH ASAMOA-CAESAR on
The Legacy of Black Wall Street;
owner, Fulton Street Books & Coffee; director of strategic advisement, George Kaiser Family Foundation

IT AIN'T NOTHING to find no starting place in the world. You just start from where you find yourself.

AUGUST WILSON (1945–2005) in
Joe Turner's Come and Gone (1988);
Tony Award– and Pulitzer Prize–winning playwright

I SET OUT to create cost-effective sutures that change color when an infection is present. . . . I definitely won't stop until the people who need these stitches actually get them.

DASIA TAYLOR on *The Ellen DeGeneres Show*; inventor and finalist in the Regeneron Science Talent Search, seeking a patent for her astounding high school invention

I WANT TO provide scholarships for young bright people so that they can graduate, get their degrees, and come out of college debt-free. Going to college for four years and coming out with a degree and, at the same time, $80,000 to $100,000 in debt puts the person behind.

CALVIN E. TYLER in the *New York Times*, February 23, 2021; senior vice president and director, UPS; former delivery driver

TALENT AND INTELLECT are universal. Opportunities and resources are not.

MICHAEL TUBBS on *Our America: Living While Black*, 2021; author of *The Deeper the Roots* (2021), mayor of Stockton, California (2016–20); founder, Mayors for a Guaranteed Income

LIKE THE MUSICIAN, a quilt maker who aspires to create great "M-provisational" compositions must focus on learning the basics of sewing and piecing quilt tops. Then they add elements of imagination and visualization that enhance their sewing.

SHERRY A. BYRD in "Jazz with a Needle and
Thread," *Fine Arts Museum Catalog*, 2021,
San Francisco;
sixth-generation Titus family quiltmaker

I REALLY DON'T want this [*Fire Shut Up in My Bones* opera] to be a token. I want it to be a turnkey.

TERENCE BLANCHARD on *PBS NewsHour*'s
"Canvas" series, 2021;
jazz musician, composer of film scores and opera,
multiple Grammy Award winner

WE COME FROM nothing, but we have a lot to give.

DAVID "BIG PAPI" ORTIZ on *Corazón de América*, 2021;
retired Boston Red Sox All-Star player, World Series
MVP (2013)

OVER THE COURSE of six decades, some six million Black southerners left the land of their forefathers and fanned out across the country. . . . The Great Migration would become a turning point in history. It would transform urban America and recast the social and political order of every city it touched.

ISABEL WILKERSON in *The Warmth of Other Suns* (2010);
author of *Caste: The Origins of Our Discontents*
(2020), winner of Pulitzer Prize for
Feature Writing (1994)

WE'VE BEEN MISLED. . . . If the majority of people who use drugs are not addicted . . . that tells you, you have to look beyond the drug itself. There are other [psycho-social factors] responsible for drug addiction. . . . That tells us we have to treat people better. We have to make sure we have social safety nets.

CARL L. HART on
The Daily Show with Trevor Noah, April 2021;
author of *Drug Use for Grown-Ups: Chasing Liberty in
the Land of Fear* (2021); professor of psychology and
psychiatry, Columbia University

LEARNING IS A daily experience and a lifetime mission. . . . The more I learned, the more I knew I had to learn. In fact, as part of your daily experience I think it is critical to understand why you are succeeding and build on it.

> BILL RUSSELL (1934–2022) in *Russell Rules: 11 Lessons on Leadership from the Twentieth Century's Greatest Winner* (2001); eleven-time NBA champion, Basketball Hall of Fame inductee (1975), author, social justice advocate

OPPORTUNITY FOLLOWS STRUGGLE. It follows effort. It follows hard work. It doesn't come before.

> SHELBY STEELE in *The Content of Our Character* (1990); senior fellow, Hoover Institution, Stanford University

THOSE WHO ARE at the head of the oppressive system know well the power of art and fear it in the hands of the people. That is why power structures throughout [human] history have sought to suppress and control the creative artist.

> CLIFF JOSEPH (1922–2020) in the *New York Times*, December 2020; artist; art therapist; co-founder, Black Emergency Cultural Coalition

GOOD MUSIC IS good no matter what kind of music it is. And I always hated categories. Always. Never thought it had any place in music.

MILES DAVIS (1926–1991) in *Miles: The Autobiography* (1989);
innovative musician, trumpet player, composer

IN *MA RAINEY*, everybody's fighting for their value, and the thing that holds us back is being Black. I wanted to show that. . . . I wanted that to be a *part* of Ma Rainey. I wanted people to see what lay in the heart of her being. Which is: *I know my worth*.

VIOLA DAVIS in the *New York Times Magazine*,
December 2020;
Oscar, Tony, and Emmy Award–winning actor

THERE WERE TIMES I wondered if I'd ever catch my first break, but . . . I kept telling myself, it'll all work out; something big is coming.

DENZEL WASHINGTON on AFI Life Achievement
Award tribute program, 2019;
award-winning actor, director, producer

THIS IS THE time when your life is revealed.
Everything is possible, but nothing is real.

VERNON REID
songwriter; guitarist; founder, Living Colour rock
band (1985); founder, Black Rock Coalition

A DREAM DOESN'T become reality through magic; it takes
sweat, determination, and hard work.

COLIN POWELL (1937–2021)
U.S. secretary of state (2001–05), four-star general,
author of *It Worked for Me* (2012) and
My American Journey (1995)

DO NOT GET lost in a sea of despair. Be hopeful, be opti-
mistic. Our struggle is not the struggle of a day, a week,
a month, or a year, it is the struggle of a lifetime. Never,
ever be afraid to make some noise and get in good trouble,
necessary trouble.

JOHN LEWIS (1940–2020) in a 2018 tweet;
U.S. representative (1987–2020); chair,
SNCC (1963–66)

IT'S ALWAYS RIGHT to be in a good fight and I am more resolute than ever. Today, tomorrow, 50 years from now, 100 years from now, that is all I am going to be doing.

MICHAEL TUBBS in the *Los Angeles Times*,
November 2020;
author of *The Deeper the Roots* (2021), mayor of
Stockton, California (2016–20); founder, Mayors for a
Guaranteed Income

HOPE IS A song in a weary throat.

PAULI MURRAY (1910–1985) on *My Name Is Pauli
Murray* (2021);
author of *Song in a Weary Throat* (1987) and *Proud
Shoes* (1956); social justice advocate; co-founder,
National Organization for Women; poet; lawyer;
Episcopal priest

THERE'S WORK TO be done off the court in so many areas in our community. Social justice isn't going to happen overnight, but I do feel that now is the time and moments equal momentum.

RENEE MONTGOMERY in her statement on leaving
the Atlanta Dream, 2020;
two-time WNBA champion; vice president and part
owner, Atlanta Dream

LITIGATION IS ONLY one tool. There certainly has to be efforts to rebuild, empower communities that have been impacted [by systemic inequalities].

> **DEBORAH ARCHER** in a February 2021 interview;
> president, ACLU national board; professor, New York
> University School of Law; author

[WHITE SUPREMACISTS] ARE lucky that what Black people are looking for is equality and not revenge.

> **KIMBERLY JONES** in "How Can We Win?" speech, 2020;
> author of *How We Can Win* (2022) and *I'm Not Dying
> with You Tonight* (2019)

PROGRESS ALWAYS NEEDS consistent vigilance.

> **TERRI SEWELL** on CNN, March 7, 2021;
> lawyer, author, U.S. representative (2011–)

AT A CERTAIN point we have to stop listening to rhetoric and start looking at results.

> **VAN JONES** on *The View*, February 5, 2021;
> CNN commentator, lawyer, author of *Beyond the
> Messy Truth* (2017)

IT IS JUST a fact that when you are trying to have people see things they've never seen before, there's going to be reluctance, if not objection to doing things differently. But you push forward and as people get to know you, they come to understand.

KAMALA HARRIS on CNN special report "Making
History," January 17, 2021;
vice president of the United States (2021–)

IT OCCURRED TO me . . . that it was an absolute necessity for me to declare homosexuality, because if I didn't, I was a part of the prejudice. I was aiding and abetting the prejudice that was a part of the effort to destroy me.

BAYARD RUSTIN (1912–1987)
recipient of Presidential Medal of Freedom (2013);
author of *Time on Two Crosses* (2003) and *Strategies
for Freedom* (1976); organizer, March on Washington
for Jobs and Freedom (1963)

THE RIGHT TO offend is about freedom of speech, and Black people in this country haven't really had the opportunity to be free. So, as a Black comedian . . . I am going to make it my business to speak as freely as I want to and have the right to offend whomever, if it's something that I stand on.

AMANDA SEALES on *Right to Offend: The Black
Comedy Revolution* (2022);
comedian, actor (*Insecure*), host (*The Real*)

IF YOU DON'T stand for something, you'll fall for anything.

SMITH HENRY CHEATHAM (1903–1973)
butcher, laborer, community organizer, social
justice advocate

NEVER BE LIMITED by other people's limited imagina-
tions. . . . You can hear other people's wisdom, but you've
got to re-evaluate the world for yourself.

MAE JEMISON
astronaut, chemical engineer, physician, author of
Find Where the Wind Goes (2001)

BEWARE THE NAKED man who offers you his shirt.

AFRICAN PROVERB

IT'S BETTER TO be prepared for an opportunity and not
have one than to have an opportunity and not be prepared.

WHITNEY YOUNG (1921–1971)
president, National Urban League (1961–71)

WAITING IS A window opening on many landscapes. . . .
To walk in the light while darkness invades, envelopes,
and surrounds is to wait on the Lord. This is to know the
renewal of strength. This is to walk and faint not.

> HOWARD THURMAN (1900–1981) in *For the Inward Journey* (1961);
> mystic; theologian; author; founder, Church for the Fellowship of All Peoples

YOU'RE EAGLES! STRETCH your wings and fly to the sky!

> RONALD MCNAIR (1950–1986)
> physicist, astronaut on the Space Shuttle Challenger (1986)

I LEARNED IN moments of humiliation to walk away with
what was left of my dignity, rather than lose it all in an
explosion of rage. I learned to raise my eyes to the high
moral ground, and to stake my future on it.

> ARTHUR ASHE (1943–1993) in *Days of Grace* (1993);
> tennis champion, social justice advocate

I BELIEVE . . . THAT living on the edge, living in and through your fear, is the summit of life, and that people who refuse to take that dare condemn themselves to a life of living death.

JOHN H. JOHNSON (1918–2005) in *Succeeding Against the Odds* (1989); founder, Johnson Publishing Company

IF YOU CAN'T count, they can cheat you. If you can't read, they can beat you.

TONI MORRISON (1931–2019) in *Beloved* (1987); author, professor, recipient of Presidential Medal of Freedom (2012), winner of Nobel Prize in Literature (1993) and Pulitzer Prize for Fiction (1988)

THERE WILL ALWAYS be moments that push us back to our faith because life has a way of reminding you that you need something bigger than you to get through a season.

T. D. JAKES on the PBS documentary *The Black Church*, 2021; bishop, The Potter's House; author of *Crushing: God Turns Pressure into Power* (2019)

WE, AS PEOPLE of faith, may not be able to stop everything that happens. But we can exacerbate what happens
if we join it, by telling a lie when we ought to tell the truth.
But we also exacerbate it if we don't say anything.

WILLIAM J. BARBER II in *The Atlantic*, November 2020;
pastor, Greenleaf Christian Church; president, North
Carolina NAACP; president and senior lecturer,
Repairers of the Breach; author

HOW IS IT that a church that emerged out of a struggle
for freedom would then indeed oppress its own [gay and
female] members? If the Black church is going to survive,
it is going to have to be welcoming to the whole entire
Black community.

KELLY BROWN DOUGLAS on the PBS documentary
The Black Church, 2021;
author of *Stand Your Ground: Black Bodies and the Justice
of God* (2015), Episcopal priest and dean of the Episcopal
Divinity School at Union Theological Seminary

WHAT WE DON'T have, we must create—a congregation that keeps the culture and the sound of the Black church, sans the homophobic and fragile patriarchy that exists in the churches that we came from.

> YVETTE FLUNDER on the PBS documentary *The Black Church: This Is Our Story, This Is Our Song*, 2021; founder and senior pastor, City of Refuge United Church of Christ; author of *Where the Edge Gathers: Building a Community of Radical Inclusion* (2005)

THE ORGANIZATION OF Afro-American Unity . . . aim[s] . . . to bring about the freedom of people of African descent here in the Western Hemisphere . . . by any means necessary.

> MALCOLM X/el-Hajj Malik el-Shabazz (1925–1965) at the founding rally for the Organization of Afro-American Unity, 1964; National Representative of the Nation of Islam; founder, Organization of Afro-American Unity

WE, AS CITIZENS, as we made our voices heard in November of 2020 by taking this country back in the right direction, we're going to have to make our voices heard the same way when it comes to legislation. . . . It's incumbent upon citizens to really make the difference.

> DON LEMON on *The Real*, 2021; CNN news anchor, author of *This Is the Fire: What I Say to My Friends about Racism* (2021)

THE WORLD CHANGES. It always changes as a result of the pressure that masses of people, ordinary people, exert on the existing state of affairs.

ANGELA Y. DAVIS in "The Herald," *Vanity Fair*,
September 2020;
professor emerita, University of California, Santa
Cruz; author of *Freedom Is a Constant Struggle* (2015);
social justice advocate

NINETEEN SIXTY-NINE WAS the pivotal year where the Negro died and Black was born.

AL SHARPTON on *Summer of Soul*, filmed in 1969,
released 2021;
author of *Rise Up: Confronting a Country at the
Crossroads* (2020); founder, National Action Network

YOUNGER FOLKS ENGAGED in this movement don't feel constrained by the losses of the past. . . . They are fearless, they are creative, and they are not deterred.

DEBORAH ARCHER in *ACLU Magazine*, Fall 2021;
president, ACLU national board; professor, New York
University School of Law; author

IN THIS ALGORITHMIC age, the logic that drives the algorithm is the ideology of white supremacy. . . . Technologies have the same biases that we do because they are built by humans.

MUTALE NKONDE on *United Shades of America with
W. Kamau Bell*, 2021;
founder and CEO, AI for the People; affiliate,
Berkman Klein Center for Internet and Society,
Harvard University

I AM TIRED of carrying this invisible burden of other people's fears.

BARATUNDE THURSTON in a 2020 TED Talk;
author of *How to Be Black* (2012), comedian,
cultural critic

CHAOS PRECEDES CREATION. . . . We're all in a birth process now.

AMARA TABOR-SMITH in a March 2021 Future
Histories Lab;
choreographer; performer; artistic director, Deep
Waters Dance Theater

POWER
CLAIMING OUR DESTINY

We're going to have to . . . recognize that our
destiny is in our hands.
MICHELLE OBAMA

THE BLACK EXPERIENCE began thousands of years before the phenomenon of white Racism appeared in human history. . . . The roots of the Black Experience . . . lie deep in the prehistory and history of the Nile Valley, the Sahara Desert, and the northern savannah lands of Africa.

ST. CLAIR DRAKE (1911–1990) in *Black Folk Here and There* (1987); professor emeritus, Stanford University; co-author of *Black Metropolis* (1945)

LAND TENURE IS the key to the Gikuyu people's life; it secures for them that peaceful tillage of the soil, which supplies their material needs and enables them to perform their magic and traditional ceremonies in undisturbed serenity, facing Mt. Kenya.

JOMO KENYATTA/Kamau wa Ngengi (1897–1978) in *Facing Mount Kenya* (1938); first president of independent Kenya (1964–78)

IF YOU WANT to go fast, go alone. If you want to go far, go together.

AFRICAN PROVERB

THERE WAS A level of cooperation in Greenwood District that was less about capitalism and more about cooperative economics.

KARLOS K. HILL on *The Legacy of Black Wall Street* (2021); author of *The 1921 Tulsa Race Massacre* (2021); chair, Department of African and African American Studies, University of Oklahoma

"WE" IS THE most important word in the social justice vocabulary. The issue is not what we can't do, but what we CAN do when we stand together.

WILLIAM J. BARBER II
pastor, Greenleaf Christian Church; president, North Carolina NAACP; president and senior lecturer, Repairers of the Breach; author

HE'D BROKEN THROUGH into a small corner of American success where his race did not curse him. Some might have lived in that space happily, rising alone. [He] wanted to make room for others. People were wonderful company sometimes.

COLSON WHITEHEAD in *The Underground Railroad* (2016); Pulitzer Prize–winning author, 2002 MacArthur Fellow

THIS "CRABS IN a barrel" is something they tell us to keep us down. Because if we link up and we share information . . . everything changes.

> YVETTE NICOLE BROWN on *Black Women OWN the*
> *Conversation*;
> actor, social justice advocate

BLACK PEOPLE. I love you. I love us. Our lives matter.

> ALICIA GARZA in a July 13, 2013, tweet;
> author of *The Purpose of Power* (2020); co-founder,
> Black Lives Matter (2013)

IT'S NOT THAT we created a movement. It was there. People were already inspired. . . . Right now we know that injustice is pervasive in our communities, anti-Black racism is a fact, and it's affecting all aspects of our lives, and we need an intervention here.

> AYO TOMETI/OPAL TOMETI in *The Cut*, March 2016;
> *Time* 100 Most Influential (2020); co-founder, Black
> Lives Matter (2013); former executive director, Black
> Alliance for Just Immigration

[Our] MISSION IS to eradicate white supremacy and build local power to intervene in violence inflicted on Black communities by the state and vigilantes. By combating and countering acts of violence, creating space for Black imagination and innovation, and centering Black joy, we are winning immediate improvements in our lives.

BLACK LIVES MATTER
founded 2013

I HAVE THE people behind me and the people are my strength.

HUEY P. NEWTON (1942–1989)
author of *Revolutionary Suicide* (1973); co-founder,
Oakland Black Panther Party (1966)

PEOPLE WHO ARE victimized may not be responsible for being down, but they must be responsible for getting up. . . . Change has always been led by those whose spirits were bigger than their circumstances.

JESSE JACKSON
candidate for U.S. president (1984, 1988); founder,
Rainbow/PUSH Coalition; author of *Keeping Hope Alive* (2019) and *Legal Lynching* (1996)

OUR GENERATION MANIFESTED Black power by integrating the American upper middle class and the historically white institutions.

> HENRY LOUIS GATES JR. on *Black America Since MLK: And Still I Rise* (2016); director, Hutchins Center for African & African American Research, Harvard University; host, *Finding Your Roots*

UP, UP, YOU mighty race! You can accomplish what you will.

> MARCUS GARVEY (1887–1940) founder, Universal Negro Improvement Association (1917)

I HOPE THIS inspires you to know that you can dream it, you can do it, you can believe, you can build anything you want.

> TYLER PERRY while touring his 330-acre Atlanta film studio; entertainment mogul, actor, writer, director, philanthropist

I KNOW OF nothing more inspiring than that of making discoveries for oneself.

> GEORGE WASHINGTON CARVER (1864–1943) in *In His Own Words*, edited by Gary R. Kremer (1987); scientist, inventor, author, "Wizard of Tuskegee"

ONE OF THE hardest notions for a human being to shake is that a language is something that *is*, when it is actually something always *becoming*.

JOHN MCWHORTER in *Stanford* magazine,
December 2020;
cranky liberal Democrat, linguist, author, cultural critic

BE SKILLED IN speech so that you will succeed. The tongue of a [person] is [their] sword, and effective speech is stronger than all fighting.

THE HUSIA: Sacred Wisdom of Ancient Egypt,
translated by MAULANA KARENGA;
creator of Kwanzaa, Africana studies scholar, author

HOW MUCH OF [one's] destiny turns on the magic of words! Words—words—words—the mark of [one's] freedom.

HOWARD THURMAN (1900–1981) in *The Greatest of These* (1944);
mystic; theologian; author; founder, Church for the Fellowship of All Peoples

OPPRESSIVE LANGUAGE DOES more than represent violence; it is violence. [It] does more than represent the limits of knowledge; it limits knowledge.

> TONI MORRISON (1931–2019) accepting the Nobel
> Prize in Literature (1993);
> author, professor, recipient of Presidential Medal of
> Freedom (2012), winner of Pulitzer Prize for Fiction (1988)

MASTERY OF LANGUAGE affords remarkable power.

> FRANTZ FANON (1925–1961) in *Black Skin, White
> Masks* (1952);
> psychiatrist, political philosopher

THE AMERICAN NEGRO must remake [our] past in order to make [our] future. . . . History must restore what slavery took away.

> ARTURO SCHOMBURG (1874–1938) in *Schomburg:
> The Man Who Built a Library* (2017);
> historian, writer, bibliophile whose collection is the
> base of the New York Public Library's Schomburg
> Center for Research in Black Culture

WE NEED TO tell the story about Jim Crow America less around what was denied us and more around [those who recognized] this as a niche opportunity. [Those who said,] "We're going to take advantage of these opportunities and build institutions, build businesses, build churches."

> CHRISTOPHER WEST on the PBS documentary *Driving While Black: Race, Space and Mobility in America* (2020); professor of history, Pasadena City College

IF ANYBODY'S GOING to help African American people, it's got to be ourselves.

> EARVIN "MAGIC" JOHNSON
> entrepreneur, Basketball Hall of Fame inductee (2002); author of *My Life* (1992)

WE'RE GOING TO have to . . . confront our own self-doubt and recognize that our destiny is in our hands.

> MICHELLE OBAMA
> First Lady of the United States (2009–17); author of *Becoming* (2018)

WE MUST LET people know that the business side [of the music industry] is so rewarding . . . to have no cutting, no editing. . . . You can just please yourself.

PRINCE Rogers Nelson (1958–2016)
musician; composer; performer; owner, Paisley
Park Enterprises

FILM IS NOT to be played with. It may be our most powerful medium and should be treated as such.

SPIKE LEE in *By Any Means Necessary: The Trials and
Tribulations of the Making of Malcolm X* (1992);
filmmaker, writer, director, author, winner of Academy Award for Best Adapted Screenplay (2019)

IF YOU WANT to be in the history of the culture, then you have to exist in the fiction; if you don't exist in the literature, your people don't exist.

WALTER MOSLEY
author of *Black Betty* (1994), *A Red Death* (1991), *Devil in a
Blue Dress* (1990), and other Easy Rawlins mysteries

NO ONE ELSE can retrieve our values and salvage our people better than we can.

DOROTHY I. HEIGHT (1912–2010)
president, National Council of Negro Women (1958–90)

WE ARE NOT a zero-sum nation, it is not you or me, it is not one American against another American. It is you and I together, interdependent, interconnected with one single interwoven destiny. When we are indivisible, we are invincible.

CORY BOOKER at the 2016 Democratic National Convention; lawyer, author, social justice advocate, U.S. senator (2013–)

FOR DIVERSITY TO become strength, the collective must be prepared to be disrupted and changed by the people around you.

JAMILA WIDEMAN in "They've Got Game," *Stanford* magazine, March 2020; member, Los Angeles Sparks (1997–2001); senior vice president of player development, NBA

WHAT WE ACCOMPLISHED in Georgia can be replicated in other states through consistent organizing, investing in state parties, and playing the long game towards victory.

STACEY ABRAMS in a February 11, 2021, tweet; lawyer; entrepreneur; founder, Fair Fight; author of *Lead from the Outside* (2018)

You can win in the South, but in order to win, you have to invest. You have such large pockets of African American voters, and the big thing is you have to persuade them that an election is important enough for them to come out and vote.

JAIME HARRISON in "Southern Strategy," *Mother Jones*, March/April 2020; chair, Democratic National Committee; lawyer; author of *Climbing the Hill* (2018)

Our goal is to increase power in our communities. Effective voting allows a community to determine its own destiny.

BLACK VOTERS MATTER

We've learned how to turn citizens into committed voters. . . . Many voters, especially Black voters, who sit out elections are not apathetic. Indeed, they are passionate about why they're not voting, and even more so about what they want from their government. It is precisely because their hopes have been unfulfilled—left to dry up like a raisin in the sun—that they choose to stay home. . . . Voting lets us choose elected officials who, in turn, make choices that affect our lives.

LATOSHA BROWN and CLIFF ALBRIGHT in "How to Turn a Person into a Voter," *New York Times*, October 2018; founders, Black Voters Matter

WHEN POOR PEOPLE feel they make a difference, they vote. There's no apathy; there's disappointment.

DOROTHY TILLMAN
talk show host; social justice advocate; member,
Chicago City Council (1985–2007)

FOR THE FIRST time, an election is not about the content of the candidates' character, it's about the content of the *voters*' character. We aren't selecting a president as much as we are proclaiming to ourselves and the rest of the world what America means.

KAREEM ABDUL-JABBAR in the *Hollywood Reporter*,
October 2020;
author of *Becoming Kareem* (2017), recipient of Presidential Medal of Freedom (2016), Basketball Hall of Fame inductee (1995)

WE HAVE TO stop letting Democrats and Republicans lead us into believing that it is their way or no way. . . . [W]e need to find a new way.

W. KAMAU BELL in *The Awkward Thoughts of W. Kamau Bell* (2017);
comedian; author; filmmaker; host, Emmy Award–winning *United Shades of America*

[BLACK POWER] IS a call for Black people in this country to unite, to recognize their heritage, to build a sense of community. It is a call for Black people to define their own goals, to lead their own organizations.

STOKELY CARMICHAEL/KWAME TURE (1941–1998)
in *Black Power: The Politics of Liberation* (1967);
chair, SNCC (1966–67); founder, Lowndes County
Black Panther Party

OWNERSHIP IS THE key. [Ownership] has changed everything in my life. I own every play, every movie, every character, every TV show. It's all owned by me. That is how I can set a path and open the door for somebody else and not wait for somebody to give me a job.

TYLER PERRY on *expediTIously with T.I. Harris*,
January 2020;
entertainment mogul, actor, writer, director,
philanthropist

I WANT US always to remember never to give our power away, but to always figure out how we can share it with somebody else.

BRITTANY PACKNETT CUNNINGHAM on *Black*
Women OWN the Conversation;
contributor for NBC News and MSNBC; fellow, Institute of Politics, Harvard University; author; social
justice advocate

I THINK ANYONE arguing for reparations and not arguing for a cash payment is racist. Racism makes you illogical. If you can inherit wealth, which we all understand, you also inherit debt.

NIKOLE HANNAH-JONES on *United Shades of America with W. Kamau Bell*, 2020;
author of *The 1619 Project: A New Origin Story* (2021),
winner of Pulitzer Prize for Commentary (2020),
2017 MacArthur Fellow

WHEN WE TALK about slavery, or the Jim Crow laws, or the Tulsa Race Massacre of Black Wall Street, we need to identify these moments as just as American as the Boston Tea Party. If we do that, if that history is brought into the present, then more citizens would understand the necessity for reparations.

ILYASAH SHABAZZ in *Elle* magazine, February 2021;
educator, co-author of *Growing Up X* (2002), social
justice advocate

PUNISHING A THIEF is not justice, it is retribution. For justice to exist, the victim must be made whole and their losses must be repaid. . . . Without restitution, there can be no justice.

MICHAEL HARRIOT in *YES! The Black Lives Issue*, Fall 2020;
senior writer, *The Root*; author of *Black AF History* (2021)

[THIS] IS A human rights organization working at the intersection of racial justice and immigration justice. Through our work we advocate for the nearly 10 million Black immigrants in the United States, while also engaging African American communities on racial justice.

BLACK ALLIANCE FOR JUST IMMIGRATION
founded in 2006

CREATIVITY IS THE supreme freedom. It is a freedom that requires discipline and rules, yet it is boundless for the person who taps into it.

ANNA DEAVERE SMITH in *Letters to a Young Artist* (2006);
actor, playwright, professor

[AFRICAN AMERICAN] SPIRITUALS are meditations on the triumph of the metaphysical over the physical realities of slavery.

KAITLYN GREENIDGE in "Black Spirituals as Poetry
and Resistance," *New York Times Style Magazine*,
March 2021;
features director, *Harper's Bazaar*; author

GOD IS ON the side of the oppressed. And since the oppressed are the ones who need to be liberated, [God] must be identified with their condition.

JAMES H. CONE (1938–2018)
founder, Black liberation theology; author of *The Cross and the Lynching Tree* (2011), *A Black Theology of Liberation* (1970), and *Black Theology & Black Power* (1969)

THE LETTERS BEHIND your name are how you make a living. The church is about how you make a life. [We] took the principles of Black theology and made it Black *practical* theology.

JEREMIAH A. WRIGHT JR.
pastor emeritus, Trinity United Church of Christ; author of *Good News! Sermons of Hope for Today's Families* (1995)

I AM NOT lucky. You know what I am? I am smart, I am talented, I take advantage of the opportunities that come my way, and I work really, really hard. Don't call me lucky. Call me a badass.

SHONDA RHIMES in an Instagram post, August 2021; television writer, producer, author of *Year of Yes* (2015)

IT IS A need of the spirit not to forget whoever has let you feel beautiful and safe. But the past is not the next amazing possibility.

JUNE JORDAN (1936–2002)
poet, essayist, professor

THERE IS GOODNESS out there and we can't be drowned in what has been curated for us to see. Find the good. It is there, and it's not hard to find.

NNEKA OGWUMIKE on *Black Women OWN the Conversation*;
president, Women's National Basketball
Players Association

ANTICIPATE THE GOOD so that you may enjoy it.

ETHIOPIAN PROVERB

THE INDIVIDUAL WHO can do something that the world wants done will, in the end, make [their] way regardless of . . . race.

BOOKER T. WASHINGTON (1856–1915) in *Up from
Slavery* (1901);
co-founder and president, Tuskegee Institute; author

THE GUYS IN our league understand the business so much more. We understand what our value is.

CHRIS PAUL in the *New York Times*, May 2018;
president, National Basketball Players Association
(2013–21); member, Phoenix Suns; author of *Long
Shot: Never Too Small to Dream Big* (2009)

THE REAL GOAL of comedy is not just to amuse us; that's there, we should be amused . . . but the best comedy, it forces us to take a second look at the society [and] at ourselves.

MEL WATKINS on "Chris Rock's *Bring the Pain,*"
Cultureshock, 2018;
author of *On the Real Side: A History of African
American Comedy* (1995)

EVERY EXPERIENCE HAS a lesson. . . . You give things power over yourself, and then they own you.

WALLY AMOS
entrepreneur; author of *The Famous Amos Story*
(1983); founder, Famous Amos cookies

THIS AWARD . . . IS for the real organizers all over the country—the activists, the civil rights attorneys, the struggling parents, the families, the teachers, the students that are realizing that a system built to divide and impoverish and destroy us *cannot stand if we do.* . . . The more we learn about who we are and how we got here, the more we will mobilize.

JESSE WILLIAMS accepting the BET Humanitarian
Award, 2016;
actor, producer

THERE ARE BODIES in the street and cops are getting paid leave and getting away with murder. . . . I am not looking for approval. If they take football away, take my endorsements from me—I know that I stood up for what is right.

COLIN KAEPERNICK in a 2016 tweet after he refused
to stand for the national anthem;
Sports Illustrated Muhammad Ali Legacy Award winner
(2017); quarterback, San Francisco 49ers (2011–16)

OUR SENSE OF self as Black people is always under attack in this society, but it's reaffirmed and enhanced at the moment you take a stance.

DERRICK BELL (1930–2011)
professor of law, author of *Confronting Authority:
Reflections of an Ardent Protester* (1994)

IN KNOWING HOW to overcome little things, a centimeter at a time, gradually when bigger things come, you're prepared.

KATHERINE DUNHAM (1909–2006)
dancer, choreographer

IT IS THROUGH the practice of goal-setting that one can compensate for life's shortcomings, whether those shortcomings be real—lack of money, limited schooling, or poor self-image—or imagined.

DENNIS KIMBRO in *Think and Grow Rich: A Black Choice* (1991);
educator, entrepreneur

IT WAS NOT the final figure in the ledger books that defined the measure of Madam Walker's life, but the promise she bequeathed to future generations that they might realize even greater successes and dream ever more elaborate dreams.

A'LELIA BUNDLES in *On Her Own Ground: The Life and Times of Madam C. J. Walker* (2001);
journalist; news producer; author; chair emerita,
board of the National Archives Foundation

IF YOU RUN, you might lose. If you don't run, you're guaranteed to lose.

JESSE JACKSON

candidate for U.S. president (1984, 1988); founder,
Rainbow/PUSH Coalition; author of *Keeping Hope
Alive* (2019) and *Legal Lynching* (1996)

MOST PEOPLE GO through life with their boat tied up next to the pier. What made me a hero was that I weighed anchor.

WILLIAM "BILL" PINKNEY

first African American to make a solo voyage around
the world (1992)

I'VE NEVER BEEN afraid to fail. . . . I think I'm strong enough as a person to accept failure, but I will not accept not trying.

MICHAEL JORDAN

first former basketball player to own an NBA team,
Charlotte Hornets;
Basketball Hall of Fame inductee (2009)

PEOPLE HAVE TO look at things for what they have, not what they haven't been given.

HAKEEM OLAJUWON

Basketball Hall of Fame inductee (2008),
NBA basketball player (1984–2002)

AMERICA IS BETTER when the Black economy is better. When the Black community is stable, it's better.

Michael Santiago "KILLER MIKE" Render in *Vanity Fair*, October 16, 2020; rapper, Run the Jewels; actor; social justice advocate

I AM THE highest-paid showrunner in television.

SHONDA RHIMES in the *Hollywood Reporter*, October 2020; television writer, producer, author of *Year of Yes* (2015)

IF YOU BELIEVE you have power, that gives you power, and if you use it, act on it, you can make things happen.

MAXINE WATERS co-founder, Black Women's Forum; U.S. representative (1991–)

AND SO, LIFTING as we climb, onward and upward we go.

MARY CHURCH TERRELL (1863–1954) co-founder, National Association of Colored Women (1896)

Now, WE AS Black people have a voice—and technology has been a huge part of that. We see things that have been hidden for years; the things that we as people have to go through. . . . I've been talking about this my whole career. It's been one thing after another.

SERENA WILLIAMS in *British Vogue*, November 2020; winner of twenty-three WTA Grand Slam titles, author of *My Life: Queen of the Court* (2009), social justice advocate

A [PERSON] WHO views the world the same at fifty as [they] did at twenty has wasted thirty years of [their] life.

MUHAMMAD ALI (1942–2016) three-time heavyweight boxing champion, philanthropist, social justice hero, author of *The Soul of a Butterfly* (2003) and *The Greatest* (1975)

[ARTISTS] MUST BE free to choose what [they do], certainly, but [w]e must also never be afraid to do what [w]e might choose. . . . We younger Negro artists who create now intend to express our individual dark-skinned selves without fear or shame. If white people are pleased we are glad. If they are not, it doesn't matter. . . . If colored people are pleased we are glad. If they are not, their displeasure doesn't matter either. We . . . stand on top of the mountain, free within ourselves.

LANGSTON HUGHES (1902–1967) in "The Negro Artist and the Racial Mountain" (1926); author, playwright, essayist, poet

I WANT MY work to be a part of justice as a whole. When I see these glimpses of strength and solidarity, it just makes me want to be better.

MICHAEL B. JORDAN actor, director, producer, social justice advocate, *Time* 100 Most Influential (2020)

ART SHOULD TAKE what is complex and render it simply. . . . I am interested in the artist who is awake, or who wants desperately to wake up.

ANNA DEAVERE SMITH in *Letters to a Young Artist* (2006); actor, playwright, professor

THE FIRST REVOLUTION is when you change your mind.

GIL SCOTT-HERON (1949–2011)
poet, author, musician, Black man dedicated to
expression of the joy and pride of Blackness

EMANCIPATE YOURSELVES FROM mental slavery; none
but ourselves can free our minds.

BOB MARLEY (1945–1981) in "Redemption Song";
musician, composer, social justice advocate

TRUE WEALTH IS having a healthy mind, body, and spirit.
True wealth is having the knowledge to maneuver and navigate the mental obstacles that inhibit your ability to soar.

RUPAUL Andre Charles in *Workin' It! RuPaul's Guide
to Life, Liberty, and the Pursuit of Style* (2010);
Emmy Award–winning host, *RuPaul's Drag Race*

WHERE IS THE power? Not on the outside, but within. . . .
Thoughts are things. You are the thinker [of] the
thoughts, that makes the thing. If you don't like it, then
change your thoughts. Make it what you want it to be.

JOHNNIE COLEMON (1920–2014)
founder, Christ Universal Temple; author of *Open
Your Mind and Be Healed* (1997)

THE SPECIALISM AND visible success of the sciences have impressed some minds to such a degree that they have virtually identified the possibilities of human knowledge with the possibilities of science.

W. E. ABRAHAM in *The Mind of Africa* (1962);
scholar; philosopher; professor emeritus, University
of California, Santa Cruz

WHEN I DARE to be powerful, to use my strength in the service of my vision, then it becomes less and less important whether I am afraid.

AUDRE LORDE (1934–1992)
Black, lesbian, mother, warrior, poet, author of
Sister Outsider (1984)

[T]HERE IS A power within us that is only activated by a conscious decision to get back up and press on. Once I realized the strength I had within myself, I began to move forward with power.

SYBRINA FULTON in "Pain to Power";
founder, Circle of Mothers [who have lost children to
senseless gun violence]

I AM AWARE that we now live in a world overrun by cruelty and destruction, and as our earth disintegrates and our spirits numb, we lose moral purpose and creative vision. But still I must believe . . . that our best times lie ahead, and . . . along the way we shall be comforted by one another.

> **HARRY BELAFONTE** in *My Song: A Memoir* (2011);
> singer, actor, social justice advocate, author

WE ARE A testament to the goodness and the grace of God. Everything in the world has tried to kill us, but we're still here. The Middle Passage tried to kill us, but we survived. Plantation life tried to kill us, but we're still alive.

> **VASHTI MURPHY MCKENZIE** on the PBS documentary *The Black Church: This Is Our Story, This Is Our Song*;
> pioneer female bishop, African Methodist Episcopal Church; author

NO EXTERNAL FORCE, however great and overwhelming, can at long last destroy a people if it does not first win the victory of the spirit against them.

> **HOWARD THURMAN** (1900–1981) in *Jesus and the Disinherited* (1949);
> mystic; theologian; author; founder, Church for the Fellowship of All Peoples

You may write me down in history
With your bitter, twisted lies,
You may trod me in the very dirt
But still, like dust, I'll rise.

MAYA ANGELOU (1928–2014) in *And Still I Rise* (1978);
poet, performer, author, social justice advocate

APPENDIX
"LIFT EVERY VOICE AND SING"
BLACK NATIONAL ANTHEM

Lift every voice and sing
Till earth and heaven ring,
Ring with the harmonies of Liberty;
Let our rejoicing rise
High as the listening skies,
Let it resound loud as the rolling sea.
Sing a song full of the faith that the dark past has taught us,
Sing a song full of the hope that the present has brought us,
Facing the rising sun of our new day begun
Let us march on till victory is won.

Stony the road we trod,
Bitter the chastening rod,
Felt in the days when hope unborn had died;
Yet with a steady beat,
Have not our weary feet
Come to the place for which our fathers sighed?
We have come over a way that with tears has been watered,
We have come, treading our path through the blood of the
    slaughtered,
Out from the gloomy past,
Till now we stand at last
Where the white gleam of our bright star is cast.

GOD OF OUR weary years,

God of our silent tears,

Thou who has brought us thus far on the way;

Thou who has by Thy might Led us into the light,

Keep us forever in the path, we pray.

Lest our feet stray from the places, our God, where we met Thee;

Lest, our hearts drunk with the wine of the world, we forget Thee

Shadowed beneath Thy hand,

May we forever stand.

True to our God,

True to our native land.

JAMES WELDON JOHNSON (1871–1938)
author, professor, poet

H₀R₀ 40, COMMISSION TO STUDY AND DEVELOP REPARATION PROPOSALS FOR AFRICAN AMERICANS ACT

INTRODUCED IN THE UNITED STATES HOUSE OF REPRESENTATIVES
JANUARY 3, 2019

This bill establishes the Commission to Study and Develop Reparation Proposals for African Americans. The commission shall examine slavery and discrimination in the colonies and the United States from 1619 to the present and recommend appropriate remedies. Among other requirements, the commission shall identify (1) the role of the federal and state governments in supporting the institution of slavery, (2) forms of discrimination in the public and private sectors against freed slaves and their descendants, and (3) lingering negative effects of slavery on living African Americans and society.

INDEX

COMMUNAL WISDOM

M

N

O

P

GRATITUDE

I am thankful daily for my family and friends because they care for, love, and support me. A special thanks to Judith Ball Thomas, who nudged me to republish *Famous Black Quotations*; and to Olivia Rynberg-Going for her masterful editing of the first draft, and to Amanda Gibson for the final polish.

Grateful acknowledgment is made to people of African descent throughout the world and through the ages who find strength in the Word.

ABOUT THE CURATOR

Janet Cheatham Bell is an author, publishing entrepreneur, re-covering academic, mom to comedian and filmmaker W. Kamau Bell (director of the award-winning documentary *We Need to Talk About Cosby*), and a grateful grandmother. Bell licensed the rights of her first two self-published quotation collections to Warner Books. Warner published *Famous Black Quotations* in 1995. Within the next seven years, she had nine books of quotations on the market. In 2013, Henry Louis Gates acknowledged her work on national television saying, "Janet Cheatham Bell is a pioneer in doing books of Black quotations." Now in her eighties, she is still writing and still taking risks.

For additional biographical information, see:
janetcheathambell.com.

JANET CHEATHAM BELL'S PREVIOUS PUBLICATIONS

Mixed Marriage: A Memoir, Sabayt Publications, 2018

Not All Poor People Are Black, Sabayt Publications, 2015

Victory of the Spirit: Reflections on My Journey, Sabayt Publications, 2011

The Time and Place That Gave Me Life, Indiana University Press, Bloomington, 2007

"The Great White Fathers' Failings," in *Black Issues Book Review*, New York, NY, May/June 2004

Famous Black Quotations® on Birthdays, Andrews McMeel, Kansas City, MO, 2003

Famous Black Quotations® on Love, Andrews McMeel, Kansas City, MO, 2003

Till Victory Is Won: Famous Black Quotations® from the NAACP, Washington Square Press, Simon & Schuster, New York, NY, 2002

Famous Black Quotations® on Mothers, Andrews McMeel, Kansas City, MO, 2002

Famous Black Quotations® on Sisters, Andrews McMeel, Kansas City, MO, 2002

"Finding My Rhythm," in *Sisterfriend Soul Journeys*, edited by Maria Dowd and Carol Smith-Passariello, PROMOTrends, Inc., San Diego, CA, 2000

Stretch Your Wings: Famous Black Quotations® for Teens
(co-author), Little, Brown and Company, Boston, MA, 1999

"Rooted Against the Wind," book review in *Black Issues in Higher Education*, New York, NY, October 1, 1998

"On Second Thought," monthly column in the *South Side Scoop*, Chicago, IL, 1997–98

The Soul of Success: Inspiring Quotations for Entrepreneurs, John Wiley & Sons, New York, NY, 1997

Literature Connections Sourcebook for The Souls of Black Folk and Related Readings, McDougal Littell, Evanston, IL, 1997

Victory of the Spirit: Meditations on Black Quotations, Warner Books (now Grand Central Publishing), New York, NY, 1996

Famous Black Quotations®, Warner Books, New York, NY, 1995

Famous Black Quotations® on Women, Love, and Other Topics, Sabayt Publications, Chicago, IL, 1992

"Myths About Homes Without Fathers," in *The Chicago Tribune*, Chicago, IL, February 13, 1990

The Black Family Reunion Cookbook, Tradery House, Memphis, TN, 1991

Famous Black Quotations® Calendars, Sabayt Publications, Chicago, IL, 1988, 1989, 1990, 1991

African Heritage Bibliography (annotated), Baker & Taylor, Momence, IL, 1987, 1988, 1989

Hispanic Bibliography of the U.S. (annotated), Baker & Taylor, Momence, IL, 1989

Famous Black Quotations® and Some Not So Famous, Sabayt Publications, Chicago, IL, 1986

"**Ethnic Studies Curriculum and Textbooks,**" in *Newsletter of the National Association for Interdisciplinary Ethnic Studies*, October, 1980

"**What Is Africa to You?**" *The Park Parent*, The Park School, Brookline, MA, February 1981

"**Teaching Ethnic Literature: Some Preliminary Considerations**" in the *Indiana English Journal*, Indiana Council of Teachers of English, Indiana State University, Terre Haute, Spring 1977

"**Challenging Racism and Sexism**" in the *Hoosier Schoolmaster*, Indiana Department of Public Instruction (now Department of Education), Indianapolis, Fall 1976

Herald the Dawn (script writer and producer, sound/slide presentation encouraging educators to include the study of ethnic minorities in their curricula) Indiana Department of Public Instruction, Indianapolis, 1976

Multi Ethnic Education (founding editor/writer) monthly newsletter, Indiana Department of Public Instruction, Indianapolis, 1976–78

With Liberty and Justice for All (annotated bibliography), Indiana Department of Public Instruction, Indianapolis, IN, 1975

My Face is Full of Your Blood (script writer and producer, sound/slide presentation to encourage educators to include the study of Africa and Black America in their curricula), Indiana Department of Public Instruction, Indianapolis, 1974

Teaching Black (co-author) African and Afro-American Studies Program, Stanford University, Stanford, CA, 1971

"Malik El Shabazz: A Survey of His Interpreters" in ***The Black Scholar***, The Black World Foundation, San Francisco, CA, May, 1970